# The Magic Mobile

Published by Addo Printing Ltd 2015 on behalf of
Sedgefield Local History Society

supported by Durham County Council and
County Durham Community Foundation

ISBN 978-0-9933227-0-9

Hi ! I'm Adam. I love history, do you ? I know you can see loads of old stuff on telly nowadays and then there's the Internet. But I've always fancied stepping back in to the past and seeing what it was really like, especially for kids like me. Well, believe it or not (and I hope you do, otherwise there's not much point in reading this book), I got the chance to do just that ! Yeah, honest !

It wouldn't have been much fun on me own, though. But I was lucky enough to meet a new friend, Cedric. Well, I say new, he's pretty old really, from way back in the past. We've been all over time together, Sedgefield's time that is. If it's history you're after, you can find many a worse place to start than Sedgefield. Mind, I'm biased, cos I live here and I think it's great.

I love people as well. Talk to anybody, me. Cedric's pretty chatty, too, but he's a bit more on the shy side. So, meeting other kids just like us, only from different times in the past, well, it beats learning about it at school ! Not that I mind school, you know. In fact, you could find this book in your school library one day. Or, better still, ask your parents to buy it for you. Make sure you let them have a look at it, too. You never know, they might learn something.

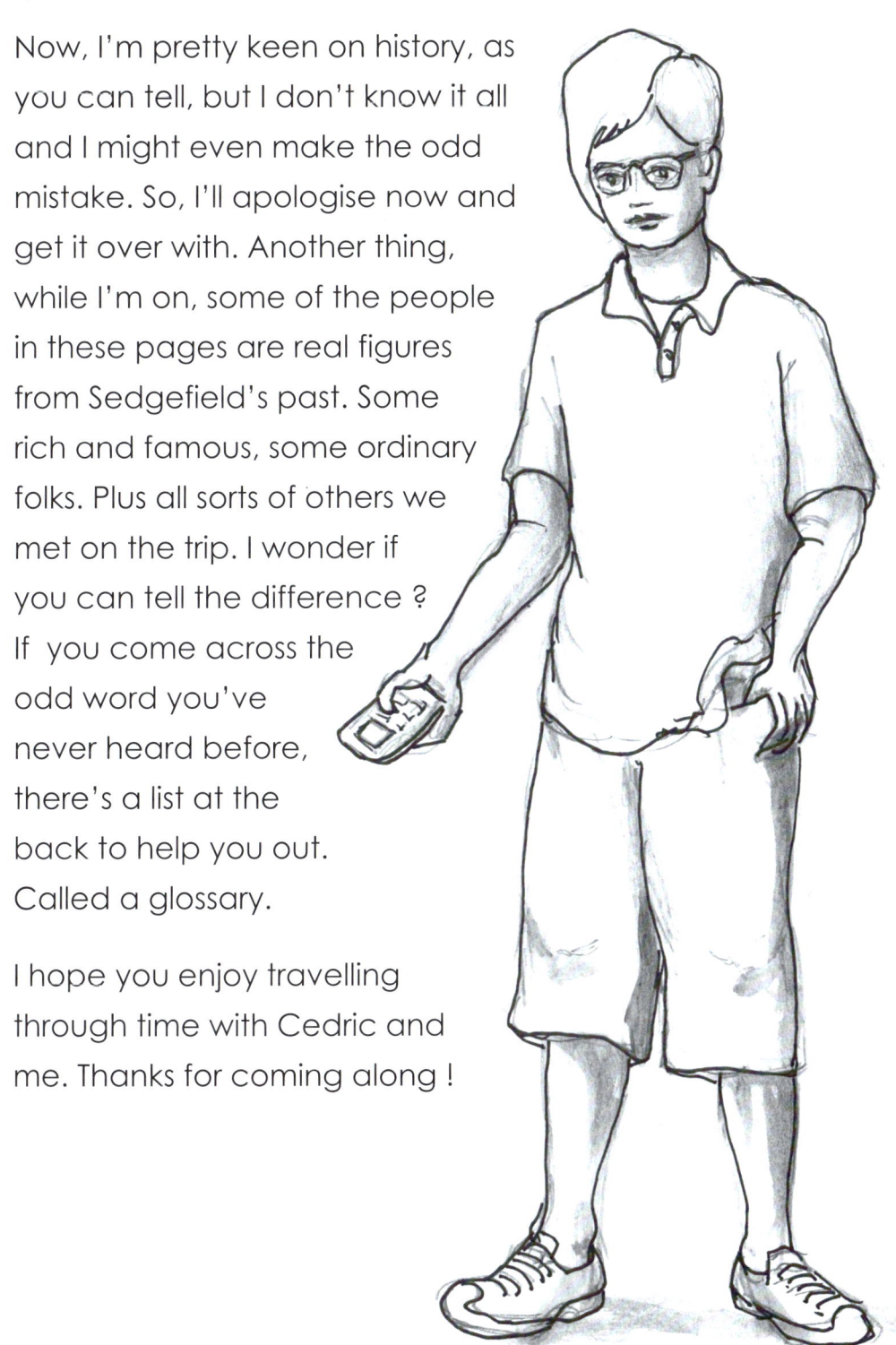

Now, I'm pretty keen on history, as you can tell, but I don't know it all and I might even make the odd mistake. So, I'll apologise now and get it over with. Another thing, while I'm on, some of the people in these pages are real figures from Sedgefield's past. Some rich and famous, some ordinary folks. Plus all sorts of others we met on the trip. I wonder if you can tell the difference ? If you come across the odd word you've never heard before, there's a list at the back to help you out. Called a glossary.

I hope you enjoy travelling through time with Cedric and me. Thanks for coming along !

# THE MAGIC MOBILE

# WOOL GATHERING

'Come on, come on, my lovelies.'

Cedric whistles, short sharp blasts, quick and bright.
He's seen his father do this many a time, learned at his
elbow. After twelve summers, he knows all the tricks.
Has to get the sheep on to good grass, away from
boggy ground, then he can take it easy, dream the
day away. Clad, as ever, in a short tunic, a soft pouch
hanging from the narrow belt round his waist. Rough
woollen breeks, wrapped around with criss-crossed
strips of cloth. Soft shoes made of animal skin, tied
round the ankles.

Face and arms bronzed by the summer sun, leaning
on his shepherd's stick, he watches over the flock with
great care. 'Come on, come on, my beauties.' The
sheep run ahead of him, their coats raggy and
matted. Bleating, shouting, rushing around, like a
crowd of starlings in search of a roost. Cedric follows
across the huge field, calling, whistling, swishing his
stick at the long grass as he goes. Cut from a narrow

tree branch, the V at the top gives just the right fit for his thumb.

At last, they reach the sweet meadow grass, well away from the muddy pools where sedge grows wild.

'Good girls, there now, don't want ye getting foot rot, do we ? Ye can eat yer fill here.'

Finding a raised bit of ground where he can keep an eye on his father's flock, Cedric settles down for some serious daydreaming. Not for long though. Within moments, he spots another young lad making his way across from the far side of the field. Jumping up, thumb stick at the ready if needs be, he bellows the full length of the pasture.

'Hey ! Ye ! What ye doing on me father's land ?'

As Cedric strides towards him, the young lad calmly raises his right hand in a friendly wave.

'What you on about ?' he smiles. Dressed for the summer weather in a pale blue polo shirt, long denim shorts and trainers, he isn't about to be chased home by a funny little lad in a smock. 'The showfield isn't private. I often cross over here. Everybody does.'

'Do they now ? Well, everybody'll be getting the

lashing of me tongue if I see them.'

Cedric leans on his stick, very sure of himself in the presence of this funny-looking stranger. His father has taught him to be fearless and stand up for himself like a man.

'Ye  live round here ? Well, then, ye should know better than to come wandering among our sheep. Me father has grazing rights across all this land you see around ye. Cedd's feld.'

'Oh, I get you. Not field. Feld ! Cedd's Feld, like Ceddesfeld, Ceddesfeld Hall !' The other lad certainly shows no fear, acting as if he'd known Cedric all his life.

'No hall round here, lad. That's where we live, that little wooden house yon side of the feld. Might not look much, but it keeps the rain out.'

'Just as well,' the stranger smiles, pointing back towards the gap in the hedge that had let him stray into Cedric's view.  'I live in a brick built house myself, over that way, in Sedgefield.'

'Sedgefield ? Never heard of it.' Cedric shakes his head. 'Mind, there is a lot of sedge round here. I have to keep the sheep out of it. No, lad, like I told ye, this place is called Ceddesfeld, after my father.'

'Fascinating,' the youngster beams, 'I'm so pleased to meet you ... er, do you have a name ?

'Course I do, Cedric, that's me, after me father, see, being the eldest. Why who's asking ?'

Grasping the surprised Cedric firmly by the hand, 'Adam,' he smiles, 'like in the Bible.'

Cedric notices a small silver box Adam had swapped over to his other hand before shaking. 'What's that ?' he asks, pointing. 'Looks like it could be worth a penny or two.'

Adam holds up his precious new phone. 'My mobile,' he says. 'They are pretty dear. Brand new, this, got it for my birthday. Twelve last week.'

'I too am of twelve summers,' says Cedric, with a gentle smile.

'Really ?' says Adam, generously passing the mobile for Cedric to hold. 'In my day, you'd be sure to have one of these. Everybody does, even little kids. I was just trying to get in touch with my mate Jonathan, over at Wynyard.'

Staring down at the mobile lying in his hand, Cedric scratches his head in disbelief. 'What ?' he sniggers.

'Ye mean ye can talk to people who aren't here ? That's handy. Better than talking to sheep all day.'

'He's not picking up, though, so I thought I'd text him instead.'

Seeing Cedric's bewildered gaze, Adam explains, 'Just a few words, you know, r u OK, sort of thing, the usual. I pressed SEND,  there was this almighty roar, a blast of air, I found myself hurtling backwards, landed here.'

'By, ye spin a good tale, lad, I'll give ye that.' Cedric shakes his head.

'No really, I knew you wouldn't believe me. I can hardly believe it myself, but honest to God ... I mean  ....' Adam grinds to a halt, for once in his life lost for words.

'Are ye telling me,' Cedric gulps for a moment before carrying on, 'that little box brought ye all the way back here through time ?'

'Something like that, yeah.' Looking as puzzled as his Saxon friend,  Adam goes on. 'When I left home this morning it was 2015. And I don't mean quarter past eight.' A quick laugh at his own joke, then he tries to explain. 'Two thousand and fifteen – this year, you know ?'

Cedric looks stunned. 'No, my friend, this is the year of Our Lord one thousand and fifteen. Now I think of it, your clothing is not of my time. Nor the strange mask on your face.'

'Mask ? Oh, you mean my specs ?' Adam laughs, whipping off his wire-framed glasses. 'Worn them since I was five. Short-sighted, see.' After a quick rub of the lenses on the bottom of his polo shirt, he holds the glasses out to Cedric. 'Have a try, if you like.'

Keeping the mysterious object at arm's length, Cedric takes a closer look. The lenses glint in the sunlight as he tips them back and forth. At last, hooking the glasses behind his ears, he slides them slowly onto his face.

'Suits you, sir !' Adam grins. 'Makes you look intelligent, like me.'

Cedric blinks, pulling a face. He stumbles slightly, reaching out a hand to steady himself.

'Make you go dizzy when you're not used to them,' says Adam, as Cedric returns the specs to their rightful owner. 'Could come in handy when you're looking for lost sheep, Cedric.'

'My eyes are sharp enough.' Cedric looks out across the feld, where his father's flock grazes, scarcely moving, their heads bowed towards the tufted grass. 'Need to be, to count sheep as good as me.'

'Can't be that difficult,' says Adam, pointing from one sheep to the next grouped around them. 'One, two, three, four, five ....'

'No, no, no,' says Cedric scornfully. 'That's not how you do it. That's ordinary numbers, sheep have special ones. Listen and I'll tell you. Yan, tan, tethera, methera, pimp...'

Trying his best to control himself, Adam lets out a great guffaw.

'What you laughing at ? I'm telling you right. Now see if you can say it.' Cedric stands back like a stern teacher, while Adam has a go. 'Yan, tan, tethera, methera, pump...'

They both break down this time, snorting with laughter. 'Pimp ! Pimp ! Not pump !' roars Cedric. 'That's what the sheep do all the time. Must be all the turnips. Don't half stink.' Grinning, the two lads try again, chanting the rhyme together. 'Yan, tan, tethera, methera...' They pause, hold each other's gaze for a moment, then finish with a loud yell, '... Pimp!'

'Not bad, son, not bad,' says Cedric, nodding like his father might. 'For a beginner, like. Then it goes sethera, lethera, hovera, dovera, dick.'

Another great splurt of laughter has Adam doubled up this time.

'There you go again. You're not taking this serious.' Cedric plonks himself down on the grass, pretending to be angry. 'I'm not telling you any more.'

'Oh go on, Cedric,' Adam tries his best to keep a straight face. 'I'm sorry, sorry, I promise I won't laugh any more, honest.'

'All right then, but I'm warning you ...' Not convinced that his pal can keep his word, Cedric carries on. 'Yan-a-dick, tyan-a-dick, tether-a-dick, mether-a-dick,' until he reaches the last number,  throws his arms in the air and yells at the top of his voice  ' – BUMFIT !'

With a great shout, they collapse in a tumbled heap on the grass, tears of laughter rolling down their faces. 'Bumfit, bumfit, bumfit,' they chant together, enjoying the silly sound. Still giggling, Cedric points at Adam, 'What's that, that music coming out your breeks ?'

Adam grabs the phone and jams it to his ear. 'Yeah ? ... What ... ? Now ? ... I'm not hungry... Aw, Mam ...' The conversation clearly at an end, Adam's hand, cupped round the phone, drops to his side. Scowling at his innocent mobile as if it was at fault, he turns to Cedric. 'Sorry mate, my mother, have to go, me dinner's ready.'

'Oh, do you have to ?' Cedric's face falls. 'You can share my dinner if you like. Only bread and cheese, but it's tasty and filling.'

Digging into the pouch at his waist, he produces a grubby bit of cloth wrapped around the simple meal he would happily share with his new friend.

'Very kind of you, Cedric.' Adam nods and smiles a little sadly. 'I'd love to stay, but my mother'd kill me if I didn't get home for the Sunday roast.' Cedric laughs as Adam goes on, imitating his mother, with a squeaky voice. 'I've been slaving in that red hot kitchen for hours. The least you can do is sit down and eat with the family once in a while.'

The lads clamber to their feet, knocking the dried grass from their clothes, neither wanting to leave the other. Trudging as slowly as possible, they set off together, towards the gap in the hedge that Adam came through earlier. Cedric prattles away as they walk.

'I'm glad my mother hasn't got one of those mobile whatyacallit things. She'd be forever calling me. Doesn't like me to be late home.'

'Tell me about it,' says Adam, dragging his feet through the tufted grass of Cedd's Feld.

'I am doing.' Cedric goes on, scowling briefly at Adam's strange remark. ' I often am, though. Late, I mean. I love sitting out in the fields. Time  floats by. All sorts of stories come into my head. Wool gathering, mother calls it. Funny that, me looking after the sheep an'all.'

They reach the gap in the hedge and stand for a moment looking back at the sheep grazing.

'This it then, Cedric. Cheers mate, nice meeting you.' Adam's out-stretched hand is quickly grabbed in Cedric's strong grasp.

'And you, lad. Pity you can't stop in my time a bit longer. I might have made a shepherd of ye yet.'

'Aye, thanks for the counting lesson.' Adam laughs. 'I'll have to teach my little sister bumfit. Sure to get her into bother.'

'You'd best be going, before you're in bother yourself.' Cedric nods towards the gap in the hedge. 'Think you can find your way back to ... what's it called ? Sedgefield ? Still sounds funny, that.'

'Hope so, I'll just ring my mam, tell her I'm on my way.' Taking the phone from his pocket, Adam glances over at Cedric.

'Tell you what, why don't you do it?'

'Me ?' Cedric looks terrified at the idea. ' I don't know how.  Never even seen one before. I might break it.'

'No, you won't,' says Adam, full of confidence in his new pal. 'It's dead easy. Look, I'll show you.'

Looking intently over Adam's shoulder, Cedric watches as his friend quickly touches one button after another, before saying, 'Now you press that one and we should get my mother.'

His fingers hover for an instant, before Cedric plucks up courage to press the button. 'Right,' he murmurs, his voice growing louder as he counts,'yan, tan, tethera !' With a final yell, he jabs a grubby finger at the shining face of the mobile.

# FAR FROM HOME

'Well, that didn't go according to plan, did it ?'
Picking himself up from the damp grass, Adam looks
round to find Cedric scrambling to his feet, both knees
grazed and a bump starting to form on his forehead.

'Are you all right, mate ?' He rushes over, taking
Cedric's elbow to help him to his feet.

'Aye, lad, just a bit winded, you know. A bit of a shock
that was. I told you not to let me touch that thing.'

'My mobile ? Where is it ?' Adam drops to the ground,
scrabbling frantically on the grass. 'Aw no, that was
just new an'all.'

'For your birthday, yes ?'

Adam nods, never taking his eyes from the vast
expanse of grass, his arms flailing in all directions trying
to find the missing phone. Cedric looks worried too. It
could be anywhere.

'Just a minute, stop.' Cedric holds up a hand. 'Do you
hear that ?'

Both boys stand still for an instant. In the distance, a faint tinkle of music.

'My ring tone ! Well done, Cedric, now all we have to do is follow it.'

Pleased with himself, Cedric falls into step beside Adam, as the two lads stride together across the field, heading towards the faint sound.

'That's good shepherding for you, see,' says Cedric, rushing to keep up with his longer legged friend. 'You may think all sheep sound the same, but they don't, oh no. I can always tell when one of them's in pain or trouble. Just by listening. Clever, eh ?'

'Very good, yeah,' says Adam, a bit sharp. 'Well, try listening now. We haven't found it yet.'

The words are no sooner out of his mouth than Cedric spots the silver case of Adam's mobile glinting on the grass. 'Yours, I think,' he says, handing over the now silent phone with a flourish.

'Thanks, mate, you've saved my life. If I'd gone home without it, my mother would have killed me for deff.'

As Adam puts the phone away in his pocket, Cedric takes a good look round. His turn to panic now. All the colour drains from his face as he says, 'Adam, I don't want to worry you, but I can't see any sheep in this field.'

Both boys stop dead in their tracks. No sight nor sound of a single sheep breaks the view or the silence hanging over the place like a storm cloud.

'Wait a minute,' says Adam after a moment. 'Where's that gap in the hedge that I came through ? That's gone as well.'

'Talk sense,' snaps Cedric, worry about his father's missing flock visible in his face. 'Do you think whoever's taken the sheep has pinched the hole in the hedge as well ?' He stomps away from Adam, too busy dreading his father's anger to listen to his friend.

'No, no, just hang on a minute.' Adams runs to catch up with Cedric. 'Don't you see what's happened ? It's done it again, my mobile. Moved us through time and space.' He stops, out of breath, scared and excited at the same time.

'Oh, aye !' snaps Cedric scornfully, 'I'm sure my father'll believe that. Sorry, I've lost the whole flock, they must be in another century.' Hopeless and helpless, Cedric drops to the ground, shouting in pain as his sore knees hit the earth. 'Hang on,' he says, feeling the wet grass around him. 'I moved the sheep away from the boggy land. How is it we're back here ?'

'That's what I'm trying to tell you, if you'd only stop bleating about your sheep and listen.' Pleased with his own joke, Adam starts to laugh. 'Ha, ha, ha, - bleating, bleating about your sheep ! That's a good 'un !' He carries on laughing until Cedric's straight face stops him.

'Yes, very funny, now stop mucking about and tell me what you mean. Where are we ? And, more important, where's the sheep ?'

Touched by the worry on his pal's face, Adam taps Cedric's shoulder and says, kindly, 'Just where you left them. Only we're in the next field – and a few hundred years back.'

Light begins to dawn on Cedric. The puzzled wrinkles disappear, his mouth drops open in amazement, before forming into a beaming smile. 'It's done it again, your birthday mobile.'

'Looks like it,' grins Adam, 'I might have to send it back. Must be faulty.'

'Or magic.' Cedric smiles broadly, his sheep – and his

father – forgotten. 'Come on then, oh wise man, where do you think we are now ?'

'Well,' says Adam, enjoying his new role as historical tour guide, 'We haven't come very far in distance, only to the next field, it's called East Park, BUT ...' Pausing for effect and to gain Cedric's full attention, he continues. 'I happen to know that, in this very spot, Time Team off the telly found Roman remains.'

Poor Cedric, totally lost now, doesn't even try to stop Adam's flow. 'It's sure to come clear soon,' he thinks, keeping his mouth shut as Adam explains.

'It was a few years ago now, 2006, I was only a little lad at the time, but my Dad brought me over to see the dig. They had these huge machines to cut the soil away. They let us look at the coins and bits of pot they found. But even better, deep down, they uncovered a Roman kiln, you know, for making pottery, almost in one piece.'

Adam is so excited telling his tale, Cedric doesn't like to ask too many questions. But he does wonder what on earth machines are. Never mind Time Team. Or telly.

'Could we be right back in Roman times ? Oh, cool.' Adam looks around for signs of life. 'Nobody about, though. Nothing. Just an empty field.'

'Not even a stray sheep,' adds Cedric, still worried about his missing flock.

'Hang on a minute,' Adam grabs Cedric's arm. 'Where's the trees ? They should be all along there. Great big ones. Leading over to Hardwick Park.'

'Maybe they haven't been planted yet !' Cedric yelps, catching up with his mate's thoughts. 'See, Adam, you're not the only one who can work things out.' Cedric shoves his sleeves up to his elbows as if he's going to wash up or something. 'If we've gone back like you say to these Roman days, we should be able to find that ... kiln thing. Can you remember where they dug it up?'

Stumped for words for a moment, Adam scratches his head and looks across the open space.

'By, you don't want much, do you ? I was only a bairn at the time. More interested in the TV cameras than the dig.'

Wasting no time on yet another word he doesn't understand, Cedric strides off, dragging Adam along with him. No buildings break the view, just the remains of low wooden fences, criss-crossing the deserted field. A straight pathway overgrown with nettles and rough grass runs through the middle. Rotting fences lead off on either side, faintly marking out blocks of land. Here and there, clods of earth specked with straw, the ghostly relics of fallen homes.

'Well,' Cedric gasps, out of breath after his dash across the deserted field, 'if we have landed in Roman times, ... where is everyone ?

Light begins to dawn on Adam. Taking a few more steps towards the far side of the field, he stops. Turning to Cedric, he holds up his hand, one finger pointing in the air. Head bent towards the ground, he thinks for a moment.

'Wait, wait, I think I know what's going on.' He stands silent, his brow furrowed in thought.

'Well don't keep it to yourself, come on, where are they all ?' Cedric hunches his shoulders, tipping both hands forward, palms up over, waiting for an answer.

'We've done the Romans at school,' explains Adam, 'and from what I can remember, they came to Britain, took over, stayed for a few hundred years then cleared off.' As he talks, Adam peers down at the ground around his feet.

'So, perhaps we've just missed them ?' wonders Cedric, folding his arms across his chest.

'Dead right, mate,' Adam replies, 'BUUUTTTT ! !' jabbing his finger towards Cedric, he adds, ' Maybe only just !'

Cedric, almost ready to give up on the Romans, stops in his tracks. 'How do you mean?'

'Well,' says Adam, darting off further across the field. 'I think I remember roughly where that kiln was.'

'Even though you were only a bairn ?' Cedric shouts, running to catch up with Adam.

'Even though I was only bairn !' Bounding ahead of his pal, Adam carries on yelling over his shoulder. 'And if it's where I think it is and it's not buried deep down in the ground, it means the Romans haven't been long gone.'

A few more strides and he stops. Cedric catches up. The two lads stand side by side.

'Bingo !' gasps Adam. A perfectly rounded stone kiln just visible through the rough grass, its long neck close to the ground. 'See, they must still have been here just a couple of years ago.'

Both boys stand in silence for a moment, gazing down at their splendid find.

'Better not touch it,' whispers Cedric, 'leave it for ... Time Team to find in your day.'

'I don't know why we're whispering,' says Adam, still in a low voice. 'There's nobody here but us.'

'Pity,' Cedric looks downcast, 'I was looking forward to meeting a Roman or two.'

'I wonder if they've left anything else.' Adam drops to his knees, feeling around in the grass. Nothing close to the kiln, not even a few broken bits of pottery. They move further off, crawling along beside the fence lines, the rotten wood home to all sorts of insects, but nothing more.

'Just a minute, what's this ?' Running his hand underneath a broken fence post, Cedric pulls out a crumpled piece of creamy coloured material, streaked with dried mud.

'Torn off somebody's toga ?' suggests Adam. 'That's what they wore in those days, a sort of tunic, a bit like yours, Cedric, only posher.'

Laughing, they put their heads together, kneeling beside each other, to take a closer look.

'What's them marks ?' asks Cedric, peering at the grubby bit of cloth.

'Looks like writing,' says Adam, growing more excited every minute.

'Oh, I get it, this isn't off a toga, it's ..., it's ... parchment. Animal skin. The Romans used it to write on.' Adam pauses, taking a moment to think how to explain that idea. ' Now, writing is putting down words so you can see them. Then you can read what it says. OK ?'

He looks hard at Cedric,

still not sure if he's understood any of this.

'OK !' nods Cedric, pleased to hear of such clever skills. 'So, what's it say ?'

'Dunno,' says Adam, glumly, 'I can't read it. I don't know what language it is, not English.'

Both boys sit back on their heels, staring helplessly at the parchment, its secrets seemingly locked in forever.

'Pity your mobile can't help out.' Cedric sighs.

'What, phone a friend, you mean ?' Adam shakes his head. 'That's off the telly, before you ask.'

'Oh, well, we'll never know what it says then.' Cedric clambers to his feet. ' Still, we found the kiln. And we've gone back ... how many years ?'

'Not sure,' says Adam, 'but the Romans left around the early fifth century, so it could be about 415 AD, as they say in the history books.'

Turning very serious for a moment, Cedric comes up with an idea. 'Why not ring 415 on your mobile and see what happens ?'

Still clutching the parchment in his left hand, Adam drags his mobile from his shorts' pocket. 'See what happens ! We could land up anywhere.'

'I hope not, not yet,' says Cedric, still unusually serious, 'I want to know what that parchment says before we flit.'

'And you think the mobile can help ?'

'Worth a try,' says Cedric, with a wry smile.

Adam does as he's told. Taps in the numbers 4 - 1 - 5. Nothing. No whoosh of air carrying them off to who knows where. No answering Hello at the other end. They don't move.

'See,' says Adam, almost glad to be proved right. 'I told you. Not a thing, zero, zilch, nada.'

'Well, of course, it can't do its magic if you don't point it at the right place.' Cedric, gaining wisdom with every moment, calmly takes the mobile and holds it over the parchment.

'Now,' he asks quietly, 'tell me what you see.'

'Wow, that's mint,' Adam holds his breath, 'How did you know it could do that ?'

Smiling broadly, Cedric replies, 'Lucky guess. If it is magic, who knows what tricks it can do ?  Now, can you tell what it says?'

'Just about, aye.' Adam still can't trust what his eyes are telling him. 'It's a bit blotchy and there's words missing, but at least it's in English now.'

The two boys huddle together, the parchment stretched out flat on the grass. Adam holds the mobile above the grimy cloth, slowly moving it along the lines of writing. Like a superpower  magnifying glass, gliding above the document, the phone transforms the words into English. Under the boys' astonished eyes, a greeting first appears.

'My dear children,' reads Adam, very quietly, still unable to believe his eyes. 'I write you while I have a moment's rest from my work.'

'Blimey,' laughs Adam, looking up at Cedric, open-mouthed. 'It's a postcard home !'

'A postcard ?' Cedric's getting used to being puzzled by most things Adam says.

'Well, more of a letter, really,' explains Adam. 'You know, letting the family know how you are when you're away from home.'

'I've never been away from home,' Cedric answers, chuckling. 'Well, not till I met you.'

Adam carries on, the ray of light from his mobile magically bringing the letter to life.

'Like the rest of this land, the weather here is very cold and wet.'

'No change there then,' laughs Adam, not taking his eyes from the parchment.

'No matter. I must serve our beloved Emperor wherever he may choose to send me.'

Adam pauses for a moment to think. 'Now, I wonder if he means Hadrian, you know, Hadrian's Wall up in Northumberland. Don't tell me, I know, you've never heard of it.'

Shrugging his shoulders, Cedric shakes his head, 'Not until I bumped into you, my friend.'

The light from his phone glowing above the parchment, Adam carries on reading.

'The broad straight road built so many years ago brought me here to this small place.'

With a quick glance at Cedric, he says, 'That'll be right, yeah, the Romans were great at building roads – dead straight, as well, didn't believe in going round if you could go over.'

Looking back at the parchment, he struggles to make out the next line. A bit smudged, the odd word missing where the parchment is torn.

'The people here, though poor, are h---d-w--- ....'

'Hardworking ?' offers Cedric.

'Aye, that'll be it,' Adam agrees, reading on. 'The people here, though poor, are hardworking, making all kinds of pottery for the  forts of Vin ...  and Se...'

Holes in the parchment stop Adam in his tracks only for a moment, before he shouts, 'I know them, been there with school – Vindolanda and Segedunum ! '

'Are they near that wall you told me about ?' Cedric asks quietly.

'Too right, mate. They're on it, whopping great forts they were. You can still see them, bits of them, anyway. They're ace.' Remembering his school trip in the summer, Adam shakes his head in disbelief.

'They must have been good builders, these ... Romans,' says Cedric, drawn in by Adam's enthusiasm. Needing little encouragement, Adam continues.

'Oh, they were, mate, brilliant. And they had toilets and baths. And central heating. Mind, they'd need it up on Hadrian's Wall, or they'd have frozen to death.'

Although he has no idea what Adam is talking about, Cedric is impressed all the same.

'Sounds ... mint,' he says, with a grin.

'You should go and see it ...' Adam rushes on. 'Oh, sorry, you can't, can you ?'

'Bit of a long trek. And  the sheep'd miss me, ' smiles Cedric, taking the mobile from Adam. 'Can I have a go ? I want to know what else this Roman has to say.' Carefully, he guides the shining light across the letter.

Adam reads on. 'So far from home, I think of you often, my dears. I will return soon, with gifts to bring good fortune - bronze am - am --- amulets...' Muddy streaks blur the words. Lifting his eyes from the letter for a moment, Adam explains, 'Amulet – that's a sort of lucky charm, Cedric.'

'To keep away evil spirits ?' asks Cedric, peering at the words he still cannot read despite the magic mobile.

'Probably,' says Adam, 'hold the phone still will you. There's only a bit more to go.'

'Bronze amulets,' he repeats, before reading on, 'in the form of animals – a goat for my dear son Aurelius, a horse for my pretty Aurora.' He pauses for a moment, then reads to the end. 'For your mother, a beautiful pendant of black jet. But not a word to her, children, this must be our secret till I return home.

Your devoted father Marcus Severus.'

The two boys gaze down at the letter, silent for once. Cedric speaks first.

'They never got that letter, did they ?'

'Afraid not,' Adam answers, a little sadly, 'I don't suppose the amulets made it back either. Time Team found some just like that buried in the ground.'

Both boys stay kneeling on the grass, looking down at the letter that had lain so long in this empty field, waiting for them to drop in.

'So, it seems they were correct,' Cedric perks up a little, 'the ... experts on the ... telly.'

'Looks like it,' smiles Adam, amused by his new pal's

easy use of words he's taught him. 'There were Romans in Sedgefield all those centuries ago. They left Britain in a hurry in the end, I know that much. Maybe he dropped this in the rush.' Adam carefully folds the letter and tucks it back underneath the little fence. 'For future historians to find,' he whispers.

# GREEN FINGERS

'Whooa ! Are you all right there, Cedric ? This is getting to be a habit. Let me give you a hand up.'

After their Roman jaunt, the boys agreed they liked time travel. Wondering where else the magic mobile could take them, Adam had tapped in 2015 and off they shot once more. This time, they'd come to earth in the fresh air like before, but this was no open field. More like a huge garden, with acres of neatly cut grass, dotted with trees and, in the distance, a lake.

'Thanks, Adam. That was a bit of a bumpy landing. We haven't come far, though, have we ?' Cedric looks around, taking in the view. 'I seem to know this place, but it looks a lot smarter. All fields in my day.'

'Hardwick Park,' says Adam. ' I come here all the time, with the Scouts mostly. We play games among the trees. I bring Buster my dog sometimes, but I have to keep him on a lead.'

Nodding to a spot away in the distance, Cedric

nudges Adam. 'Eyup, we've been spotted. See that lad making straight for us ? Looks like we're finished afore we start.'

'I don't know,' says Adam. 'He looks friendly enough. Howay, let's say hello.'

'Aye, well don't blame me if we end up in the lake for our pains.'

Cedric stands nervously beside Adam as the other lad makes his way steadily towards them. 'Good morning, gentlemen.' He certainly doesn't look frightening, in his soft simple clothes, layered to keep the heat in. A simple white shirt under a loose waistcoat of dark red, buttoned to the neck, with two deep pockets along the bottom edge. Over that, a grey jacket hangs loose and comfortable, its wide cuffs turned back with three smart buttons. Earthy coloured trousers tuck in to long brown gaiters, like boots.  Taking off his soft black hat, he bows his head slightly, hands behind his back. Smiling, he asks, 'Are you here for the garden tour, gentlemen ?'

'Sounds interesting,' says Adam, smiling confidently. Very uneasy, Cedric looks to Adam for support. 'I'm with him,' he stammers, 'we'll clear off again, if you like, I only live over the fields.'

'And a few hundred years ago,' Adam adds, laughing. Seeing puzzlement on the other lad's face, he explains. 'You might not believe this, but me and my mate Cedric here, we kind of dropped in by mistake.'

'Have you come far ?' the other lad asks.

'You could say that,' nods Cedric, a bit more sure of himself, now he hasn't been chased or told off.

'We're both from Sedgefield right enough,' says Adam. 'Only not from the same part. Or the same century.'

The other lad furrows his brow. 'Well, not to be rude, you know, but  you do look a bit odd.'

'Hey, steady on,' says Cedric, his right hand flying up. 'We could say the same about you.'

Jumping in quickly, before the hand becomes a fist, Adam smiles at both lads.

'Don't mind Cedric, he's a bit touchy. I'm Adam, by the way.'

'Pleased to meet you.' The garden lad nods, shaking hands with Adam, copying the words and actions of his betters at the big house. 'And you, Cedric,' he adds quickly, grabbing the hand of the startled young shepherd. 'I'm Jack, aye, Jack of all trades. Mind, I've nearly forgotten my real name now. Often, I just get 'lad' or 'you boy'.'

All lads together now, Adam asks, 'Now, Jack, before we go any further, let us in on a secret, will you ? Last time we looked it was Roman times, so what year are we in now ?'

'1780, my friend, two years to the day since I came to work here at Hardwick Hall.' Jack stands tall, holding on to the edges of his tunic jacket, just like the older men he works with. Sounding just like them too, he goes on, 'Aye, ten year old I was when I started here.'

Looking each other straight in the eye, the other lads chorus, 'Same age as us !'

'Never !' says Jack, surprised that these two skinny scraps are twelve years old like him.

'I had to leave home to make way for the rest of our tribe,' he goes on. 'They're only at Bishop Middleham, though, so I can walk home to see them once in a while. Our Betsy comes wi' me sometimes, if we have a day off together.'

He stops suddenly, his eyes taken by someone moving nearby. 'Oh, no,' he says, 'Talk of the devil. Here she comes. She'll be checking up on me. Worse than my mother.'

Jack falls silent as his sister marches towards him, her long brown skirt rustling around her feet. A soft white blouse, ruffles of lace at the neck and sleeves, is covered by a pretty tunic, the colour of straw. A huge apron protects the long skirt and a neat little cap of white cotton sits on the back of her head.

'I hope you've given your neck a good scrub, our Jack. You don't want a tide mark on your good shirt.' She whips a large hanky from under her tunic, spits on it and wipes Jack's face all over. Even behind his ears.

'Give over, our Betsy,' shouts Jack, squirming out of his sister's grasp. 'I've already had a good wash. Showing me up in front of visitors.'

'What you talking about, visitors ?' she snaps, licking her fingers to smooth down his hair. 'No visitors here yet. Nobody to see you but me, just as well.'

Adam and Cedric glance sidelong at each other. Jack says nothing, as Betsy prattles on. 'I can't stand wasting time with you. I'm due at the top gate to meet Lady Hamilton. You'd best get about your business, if you know what's good for you.'

Off she stalks, leaving the three lads speechless, watching her bustle away. After a moment, Jack recovers enough to explain. 'My big sister. 17 years old. Thinks she's my mother.'

'She's worse than mine,' smiles Adam, ' Talk about bossy.'

'She's been practising her curtsey all week, so she can meet Lady Hamilton when her carriage pulls up at the gate,' says Jack, ruffling his slicked-down hair and plonking his soft black hat on top.

' I'm glad she didn't start on me,' says Cedric, relieved to see the back of Betsy.

'Don't you realise, Cedric,' says Adam, his face beaming. 'She didn't start on you, 'cos she didn't see you. She didn't see either of us.'

''Nobody to see you but me,'' Jack recalls.
'I wondered what she meant.'

Pulling himself up to his full height and rubbing his hands in glee, Adam declares, 'Well, Cedric, I think the magic mobile has just revealed another of its little tricks.'

Both Cedric and Jack look equally puzzled until Adam, throwing both hands in the air, cries 'Invisibility !'

The two other lads stand silent as he races on.

'Don't you see, either Betsy is very rude and just ignored us ... OR ! she couldn't see us.'

Pacing around as he talks, Adam tries to figure out what's going on, so that he can explain to his two dumbstruck mates. They stand gaping open-mouthed, as he thinks aloud. And very fast.

'Jack can see us fine, so it doesn't work on everyone.' He sweeps round to face the others. 'Sorry, Jack, should have told you before. Me and Cedric landed here thanks to my mobile, which seems to have magic powers of time travel. And now, looks as if it makes us invisible too.' Adam comes to a sudden halt. Cedric and Jack look at each other, their eyes locked in disbelief. 'Well, the sheep didn't seem to notice you,' says Cedric at last.

'Just a minute,' Jack holds both hands in the air, in front of himself, like a shield against Adam's bombardment of ideas. 'One thing at a time might help.'

'Quite right,' agrees Cedric, 'I bet you don't even know what a mobile is. I didn't until Adam told me. Clever things, you know. You can talk to people who aren't there.' He nods wisely, as if he'd been using a mobile all his life.

'But this one seems to have a will of its own,' adds Adam, taking the phone from his pocket. 'It won't let me ring home, but it can carry us through time, read other languages, make us invisible ...'

'Could come in handy,' says Cedric, handing the mobile across for Jack to have a look.

'Invisible ?A bit like me at Hardwick,' Jack joins in. 'You're supposed to stand back and say nowt, see. So, the gentry forget you're there. You hear all sorts.' He stops, gazing down at the strange silver box in his hand. 'And now you tell me this little device does the same for you ?'

'Looks like it,' says Adam, grinning. 'Your scary sister couldn't see us anyway.'

'I know,' Jack laughs at the memory. Pinching his lips and waggling his head as if his neck was on a spring, he drops easily into his sister's piping voice. 'Nobody to see you but me.'

'Brilliant !' Adam claps his hands in glee. 'The spit of her !' agrees Cedric, grinning broadly.

'Anyway,' Jack smiles, jamming his soft hat back on his head, 'I've got work to do, can't stand around jawing all day. I'd better get cracking up to the glasshouse. Are you coming?'

As he sets off smartly, it only takes a moment for the two lads to glance at each other and nod in agreement. 'You're on,' agrees Adam, at home already with this stranger. He and Cedric gallop along, struggling to keep up with Jack's long strides. 'If you stick with me and keep quiet,' he says, enjoying being in charge, 'you being invisible like you say, you could tag on to the garden tour with the visitors.'

'Cool,' says Adam. 'Now Cedric, remember, keep your gob shut and we'll find out all sorts.'

'My lips are sealed,' grins Cedric, dragging a grubby finger across his mouth.

As they walk, Jack tells them about his work at Hardwick, glad to have the chance to show off a bit. 'Well, there's no sittin' about, I can tell you that,' he says. 'Boot lad, that's me main job, you know, polishing all the boots and shoes. But I do all sorts, whatever I'm told, really.' Taking a long breath of fresh air, he goes on. 'This is where I like to be though, out in the gardens. Among the trees and plants.  There's a lot to learn, but Mr Croft, he's the head gardener, says, if I keep my nose clean and watch and learn from him, I'll be doing all right.'

'You could have his job in a few years time,' jokes Adam.

'Aye, you never know,' smiles Jack. 'My father reckons I've got green fingers. You know, good in the garden. Anyway, Monday last, when I collected Mr Croft's Sunday best boots from the glasshouse for cleaning, he says ... '

Wagging his finger, Jack puts on another, older, gruff voice. 'Now then lad, if you work hard all week and get a shine on them boots I can see me face in, I'll let you come round with us on open day, while I show the visitors round.'

'You should be on the telly,' laughs Adam, as Cedric shakes his head, as if to say, 'Don't ask.' Wrapped up in telling his tale, Jack simply shrugs. ' Why, I couldn't believe me luck ! I had a job to hold on to his boots, I was shaking that much.'

Still striding ahead, his tongue loosened by having two new pals to share his excitement, Jack rushes on with his story. 'I thought the week would never end. I polished every boot in the house. You could have hung them on the wall for mirrors.'

'And were they good enough ?' blurts Cedric.
'Did he say yes ? Mr Croft ?'

'Well aye !' beams Jack proudly. 'That's where we're off now. To meet him. Howay get a move on. No running, mind, it's not allowed, just walk as fast as you can.' Striding onwards, he takes the final few steps towards the glasshouse, Adam and Cedric bustling breathlessly behind.

# THE GARDEN TOUR

'Ah, there you are, Jack, I'd nearly given you up.' Head gardener Mr Croft steps out from the doorway of the glasshouse. His buckled shoes, so carefully polished by Jack, gleam in the sunlight. White stockings tuck into his knee breeches. He brushes his hands down the front of his long buttoned tunic, tapping the huge pockets, emptied now of his usual gardening paraphernalia. Rolling down the sleeves of his white shirt, he is ready for an audience.

'Come along now, look lively. Visitors will be arriving. Now remember, what I said, I want you to make sure the visitors stay together and keep up.'

'Yes, Mr Croft,' Jack nods, 'And make sure they don't snip bits off your best plants.'

'That's right, good lad, you can't be too careful. I haven't got eyes in the back of my head.'

'Just as well,' Cedric starts sniggering, until Adam's

sharp elbow in his side shuts him up.

Mr Croft puts on a soft black hat almost identical to Jack's. Rubbing together his big hands, roughened by years of gardening, he strides off. 'Now, follow me lad, time to get to work.'

'He hasn't spotted us,' whispers Cedric, as he and Adam fall in at either side of Jack.

'Let's hope the magic keeps working.' Adam murmurs.

'Quiet you two,' Jack hisses out of the corner of his mouth. 'And no giggling when Mr Croft puts on his posh voice.'

'Good morning, ladies and gentlemen.' Mr Croft doffs his hat to the group of about twenty visitors eager to see the gardens. 'Welcome to Hardwick Pleasure Gardens. I shall conduct the tour this morning and my young garden boy Jack will bring up the rear, as it were.'

Jack gives a nervous smile and slight nod to the visitors, hoping they can't see Adam and Cedric, standing like a pair of bookends either side of him.

Mr Croft continues, 'Now, I know you'll be very impressed by all the plants you see on our tour today, but I must insist you refrain from taking any samples home with you.'

A few ladies giggle, others look distinctly huffed that the gardener could suggest such low behaviour. A few busy themselves putting up parasols to keep off the sun.

'Finally, may I ask that you remain with the group and keep to the paths at all times.'

So saying, Mr Croft sets off ahead of his willing followers, scattering information as he goes.

'So far, so good,' whispers Cedric, 'they can't see us.'

'Good old magic mobile,' Adam adds quickly before Jack shushes them both with a look.

'Our tour begins here, on the Grand Terrace,' says Mr Croft proudly, sweeping his arms open and then forward for emphasis. 'Eight yards wide, 560 yards long.  Very impressive, I think you'll agree. Leaving the Hall behind us, we proceed towards the lake. 40 acres of water all told, complete with a dam and two beautiful cascades.'

Mr Croft sets a fair pace and the visitors have to step out to keep up with him.

'The circuit walk we are taking today covers the entire pleasure grounds of Hardwick. The parkland is cleverly laid out, as per Mr Burdon's instructions, to provide changing vistas round every corner.'

The group continues along the terrace, passing the Gothic Seat with its three arches.

'Modelled on the choir screen at Gloucester Cathedral,' Mr Croft tells the visitors, as they continue toward the Bathhouse, Jack's two invisible pals stuck to his sides like limpets. True to their word, they don't utter a sound, unlike some of the ladies in the group as the Bathhouse comes in to view.

'Oh, look, Matilda !' 'How heavenly !' 'Isn't it sweet ?'

Mr Croft points out the elegant columns creating an open portico at the front. On either side, as well as a bedroom and breakfast room, changing rooms for visiting ladies and gentlemen.

'The Bathhouse is modelled on the Roman style,' Mr Croft explains. Adam and Cedric nudge each other, but speak not a word. 'Complete with images of gods,' continues the tour guide, unaware of the two stowaways taking in his every word. 'Guarding the door, Diana, goddess of hunting. In one dressing room, a sculpture of the head of the sea god Neptune, in the other a painting of Apollo playing his lyre.'

The crowds nod their approval of these classical touches. Even Cedric looks impressed, especially now that he knows just who the Romans were. Adam puts a warning finger to his own lip as Mr Croft continues.

'Water from the lake is used to fill the circular bath, which is lined with blue mosaic tiles. The effect is most pleasing. One could almost imagine oneself in Italy.'

Further squeals of delight from the young ladies in the group are hushed by Mr Croft's raised palm.

'The window above, set into the domed roof, allows light to fall on to the water, making the bath seem even deeper. Finally,' he announces, with a flourish of his right hand, 'please note, over the door, the owner's coat of arms, carved in stone. Mr Burdon is very aware of the health benefits of bathing.'

'All right for him,' whispers Jack, 'but George, the valet, has to stand outside and freeze, looking after the master's clothes while he takes his early morning dip.'

Jack's two shadows snigger. Mr Croft glances towards the back of the group.

'Did someone have a question ?' He peers over the heads of the visitors, all too meek to dare interrupt his flow.

'No ? Very well. Let us continue towards the first of our many follies. As you may know, garden follies have become very popular with gentlemen and ladies of the upper classes.'

'All the rage with toffs, they are,' Jack tells two young women near the back of the group. 'They like pretending they've been there for ages, when they're brand new really. They say some of them were built with stone from the old manor house, though.'

His enthusiasm loosening his tongue, he stops when he sees Mr Croft glaring from the front of the group.

'I'll thank you to keep quiet, young man. Just remember who's the expert around here.'

'Yes, Mr Croft, sorry, Mr Croft.'

Jack looks suitably shame-faced, unlike his two pals, silently laughing their heads off.

As Mr Croft leads on, the three lads hang back a little from the rest of the group.

'He goes on a bit, old Croft,' says Jack, 'but he's told me all about the follies. Shall I give you the potted version ?'

'Good idea,' Cedric nods. 'What do you think, Adam ?'

'Fine by me,' Adam agrees, 'but won't Crofty notice you talking away to the fresh air ?'

'If we keep well back, I doubt he'll notice. He's a bit deaf anyway,' adds Jack. 'He'll be so busy spouting, I could fall down a rabbit hole and he'd not miss me.'

'Like Alice in Wonderland,' Adam jokes. Seeing the

puzzled faces of the other two, he tries to explain. 'Sorry lads, after your time. It's a story, for kids, you know. She had loads of adventures down a rabbit hole.' Cedric smiles, quite happy to accept anything Adam cares to tell him about his strange and surprising world.

'You've lost me, mate,' says Jack, keeping an eye on Mr Croft and his group. 'Now, follow me, but stay back from the crowd and, for goodness sake, keep quiet.'

Ahead of them, the visitors keep disappearing from view, as the winding path takes them deeper into the woods. Finally, the group stops at a clearing in the trees.

'Right, lads, we'll hang back here,' says Jack, proud of his status as guide to his own little group. 'This is close enough. Can you see, look, that's the first of Mr Paine's follies. The Bono Retiro. I'm told it means place of pleasant retirement.'

The boys stand open-mouthed, amazed to find such a splendid building in the middle of woodland. A mirror placed at the entrance, opposite the cascade, reflects the tumbling water.

'I've never seen anything like that in all my life,' gasps

Cedric, almost dumb-struck.

Adam, his voice barely a whisper, asks, 'All those arched windows and stained glass. Is it a church ? '

'A library,' says Jack, 'but the books are all just painted on. Most visitors aren't allowed inside. Only honoured guests,' he explains, breathing hard on the H in his best Mr Croft voice.

'Like Lady Hamilton ?' asks Adam, with the same heavy huh. 'I hope your Betsy did a god job helping her out of her carriage.'

'Aye,' says Jack, stepping back to take in the view. 'She'll be having her own private tour with Mr Burdon. Can't expect her to muck in with the local yokels.'

'It's brilliant,' sighs Adam, 'pity it's not there any more, the Bono Retiro. Well, not much of it, anyway.'

'Why, what happened to it ?' asks Cedric, puzzled.

'Oh, you know, kids mainly, mucking about. People came and stole bits of stone and things over the years.' Adam looks embarrassed, even though he wasn't responsible.

'That's a sin and a shame !' Jack has to stop himself

from shouting out loud. Mr Croft and the visitors are just out of earshot if they talk quietly. 'Fancy wrecking a beautiful building like that. They should have more respect.'

'You're right there, Jack.' Cedric puts a friendly arm round his new pal's shoulder. 'They'd have had their hands stuck in the fire in my day. Times seem to have changed a little.'

'I know, I know, you're both right, I agree, it's terrible.' Adam goes on to explain. 'A lot of these follies were damaged over the years, vandalised. But some of them have been restored. In my day, Hardwick Park looks nearly like it does in yours, Jack.'

Whipping out his mobile, he shouts, 'Tell you what, let's have a selfie while we're here !' Turning his back to the building, Adam stands in the middle, Cedric and Jack astonished on either side. Holding the phone in his right hand, giving a thumbs up with his left, 'Right, lads, smile !' Click ! A moment later, their photo appears on the mobile screen.

Cedric steps back in surprise, as Jack leans in to take a closer look. 'Smart portrait,' he says, beaming proudly, 'Just like the gentry – only quicker painted ! I feel like Mr Burdon of Hardwick Hall himself.' Standing tall, he grasps the edges of his tunic. Taking on the resonant voice of his master, he asks, 'Now gentlemen, shall we proceed ?'

Grinning, the three lads fall smartly in to step, Jack in the middle, back in charge of his two new mates.

'Tell us about  this Mr Burdon, Jack ?' says Adam,  as they walk. 'Bigwig round here, is he ?'

 Striding on, Jack tells them, 'A real gentleman, Mr Burdon, even though he's from South Shields. And talk about family – youngest of seventeen ! His father made a fortune from coal mining. Left Mr Burdon £40,000. A lot of money in 1748. That's when he bought Hardwick.'

As they follow the path away from the Bottle Pond, named for the shape it makes, Jack tells them, 'Getting a bit skint now, though, Mr Burdon. Can't afford to build the big new house he was so set on, bigger even than Hardwick Hall. Mind, I'm not surprised, he's spent a fortune on the gardens and follies.'

As they round the edge of the lake and the path straightens out, Jack smiles. 'We're coming to my favourite now, right high up on a mound. Looks lovely when the sun's on it. There, see ?'

All three stop, heads tipped back, eyes blinking in the bright sunshine. A vivid blue sky provides the perfect backdrop to a majestic building of pure white stone. Elegant, rounded  pillars stand on all four sides, creating a covered walk. A domed roof completes the image.

'The Temple of Minerva,' beams Jack. 'Built by Master Mason John Bell of Durham, 1757.'

'I hope your lot haven't wrecked it,' Cedric looks across to his 21st century pal.

'Just the opposite.' Glad to have some good news, Adam explains. 'It looks exactly the same now, since it was restored. Makes a great photo. Look, the visitors are heading up there with old Crofty.'

Diving back into his pocket for the mobile, he hoists it into the air, poised for a quick pic. 'Gotcha !' he shouts gleefully, forgetting for an instant the rule about keeping quiet. The other two lads round on him, their shushing almost as loud as his yell. All three bob down together, huddled in a giggling heap. From their open hiding place, they watch the distant group admiring the temple, gleaming white in the afternoon sun.

'They sometimes stop there for tea,' Jack whispers. 'We'd better keep out of sight and sound.'

As they stroll along, keeping the visitors in view, Jack tells the boys about the elaborate plaster carvings on the temple ceiling. Italian artists added painted scenes from Roman legends.  Around the wall stand busts of famous men from the past. Above the door, a carving of Minerva, goddess of wisdom, who helped Perseus slay the Gorgon Medusa.

'None of that left now, I'm afraid,' admits Adam, ruefully, 'but at least the Temple's still beautiful on the outside.'

'What about the Gothic Bridge and the Statue of Neptune ?' asks Jack, dreading the reply. 'Both still standing, I'm pleased to say,' Adam announces triumphantly. 'Mind you, the bridge did fall into the Serpentine and had to be rebuilt in the 1990s.'

'What about that chap Neptune ?' asks Cedric.
'Is he still about ?'

'Not the original one, sadly.' Adam explains. 'Vanished during the 1940s.  The Hall was used by the army during the war, see. Seems one of the officers fancied old Neptune for his garden pond. But the new one is just as good as in your day, Jack.'

As the visitors emerge from the Temple, the lads follow at their usual distance, heading towards the Gothic Bridge. There they stand for a moment, admiring the bronze statue of Neptune, the sea god, standing on his plinth, his foot on a dolphin, a trident in his right hand. 'Just like in my day,' smiles Adam.

'Now, ladies and gentlemen, let us proceed to the Gothic Ruin.' The calm air clearly carries Mr Croft's words towards the boys, still keeping their distance from the visitors group.

'Ruined already ?' says Cedric. 'Have your lot been here before us, Adam ?'

'Not this time,' Jack explains. 'It was built that way, it's all the fashion at the moment, ancient history. Makes the owner look more important. They don't mind pinching stones from here and there either.'

'So it's not just in your day then, Adam,' says Cedric, before Jack goes on.

'They say Mr Burdon fetched stones from Guisborough Priory. His niece is married to the owner, so they seemed to think it was all right to chop bits off an ancient building.'

Jack keeps his voice low; he knows Mr Croft wouldn't be too pleased to hear him giving away family secrets. By the time the boys reach the round tower, several visitors have climbed the spiral staircase inside.

'It would be great to do that,' says Adam, 'I bet you get a brill view across the park.'

'Have you never climbed it then ?' asks Cedric. 'Not even with your, whatyacallems ... Scouts ?'

'No steps there in my day,' explains Adam, 'but the tower has been rebuilt, just like this.'

'Seems mad, in your day - one lot knocks it down, another has to build it up again.'

More puzzled than ever by the goings on in Adam's time, Cedric sits down on a grassy bank.

'May as well take it easy for a while,' he says. 'They're going to be ages up and down them steps in their long robes.'

'Pity the visitor centre isn't built yet,' smiles Adam 'We could have had an icecream.'

He and Jack settle down beside Cedric, enjoying the summer sunshine. Not for long, though.

'CEE ... DRIC ! CEE ... DRIC !'

Jumping to his feet, thumbstick at the ready, Cedric peers in to the distance, wheeling round to look over both shoulders in turn.

'What was that ? Did you hear that ?' He looks skywards, suddenly edgy and nervous.

'What ? I never heard anything,' says Jack, keeping his eyes on the visitors and Mr Croft.

'Only those silly girls giggling at the top of the tower,' adds Adam, stretching out on the cool grass.

'My name, somebody called my name.' Still on his feet, Cedric looks worried now.

'Don't be foolish,' says Jack. 'Nobody knows you're here. And they wouldn't know your name even if they could see you.'

'I'm telling you,' Cedric insists. 'Somebody called my name. It was my father. He'll tan my hide if he sees I've left the sheep. I'll have to go back.'

He starts walking away from the others. They dash after him.

'We haven't finished the tour yet,' Jack protests, grabbing Cedric by the arm.

'Sorry, Jack,' says Cedric, gently removing the young gardener's hand from his arm. 'I'd love to stay longer, but if I don't get back to that feld double quick, I'm dead !'

All three lads look worried now. Adam fumbles in his pocket for his mobile.

'Right,' he stammers. 'Right ... well ... the thing is ...'

'Never mind humming and haaing,' Cedric snaps, 'Press some buttons and get me back home. We only have to cross in to yon pasture.'

'Aye – and through several hundred years,' says Adam, frantically tapping at the phone. Nothing.

'Sorry, Cedric. I don't know what numbers got us here, never mind how to get back.'

'How about 2015 ?' suggests Cedric in desperation. 'There seems to be something magic about that number.'

'Worth a try,' agrees Jack. 'You'll have to do something, Adam, the visitors are moving on. I'd better catch up.'

'OK,' says Adam, not convinced, but he has no other ideas. 'Here goes. 2 – 0 – 1 – 5.'

In an instant, a great whooshing sigh lifts Cedric into the air. Adam grabs his foot, clinging grimly to his mate as they float ever upwards.

'I didn't know you were coming as well,' laughs Cedric.

'Looks like it,' Adam grins up at him. 'You don't get rid of me that easy.'

'Just don't let my father spot you, that's all.'

More confident now they are airborne, the two lads take a last look back at the parkland below. On the ground, Jack looks sadly up at his two new friends, floating away together.

'You can't go yet !' he calls, waving both arms, criss-crossing in front of his face. Torn between laughter and tears, he shouts, 'You haven't seen the Banqueting House !'

'Maybe next time,' yells Adam. 'Thanks for the tour.'

'It was mint !' adds Cedric, raising his thumbstick in a last farewell.

# ALMSHOUSE BROTH

'Hang on, Cedric ! Coming in to land !'

The two lads cling together, with Cedric's thumbstick as a mast, his smock a sail billowing in the wind. Thud ! They land heavily, falling at once into a tussling heap.

'Owya !' yells Adam, rubbing at his grazed knee. 'At least I haven't ripped the shorts, thank goodness. Me Mam'd have me life.'

'Now where have you brought me ?' Straightening his smock, Cedric looks up, puzzled to see buildings all around. In front of them, a wide strip of black divides the street in two. A church tower rises behind a neat row of tiny houses. 'Not much like my father's feld.'

As the two lads scramble to their feet, they hear giggling, then a cheeky yell.

'You could hurt yourselves mucking about like that.'

Three girls on the other side of the road, laughing so much at the boy's surprise arrival, they have to hold each other up. They're all wearing cotton dresses with cardigans, short white socks and soft black canvas shoes. Behind them, a butcher's shop, its little bay window crammed full of cuts of meat, piled high. Sides of bacon and beef hang down from huge curved hooks.

'Leave this to me, Cedric. Don't worry, I know where I am. Front Street. That's the parish hall behind us, hasn't changed much. St. Edmund's, the church, same as ever.' The lads start to cross over the road, towards the girls, pretty sure now that only other kids can see them. No adults about, anyway. Looking around as they walk, Adam sighs 'Oh cool ! The almshouses.  I've only ever seen them in old photos.' Dropping his voice as they get closer to the girls, he whispers, 'Say nowt, but by my day, this is the Indian takeaway, Pizza Castle next door.'  Cedric, more used to seeing animals walking around a field than hung up by their feet, pulls a face as he gets a closer look at the butcher's window.

'Well, you're a funny looking pair, I must say.' One of the girls seems to be in charge.

'Nice of you to drop in,' her friend adds, setting them all off again, giggling.

'No problem,' Adam smooths down his shorts and adjusts his glasses, behaving like the action hero he'd love to be. 'I'm Adam, this is Cedric.'

More spluttering from the girls. 'Cedric ! What kind of name's that ?' says one, grinning. 'And why are you wearing a frock ?' Another points a mocking finger at Cedric. They're almost helpless with laughter now. Cedric glares at them, his face scarlet with rage.

'As a matter of fact, it's his work uniform,' says Adam, calmly, 'he has very important job working on the land.' For a moment, the girls are stunned into silence, before one pipes up.

'Working ? You can't be old enough.'

Standing tall now, his face restored to its usual pallor, Cedric leans on his thumbstick.

'Oh yes,' he says, proudly, 'father says a lad of twelve summers is quite old enough to tend the flock.'

Puzzled by Cedric's way of talking as well as his clothes, the girls glance at each other. 'Same age as us,' they chorus, before the smallest one adds, 'but we're still at school.' Her mate, a little more sure of herself, goes on. 'You're not from round here are you ?'

'Indeed I am,' snaps Cedric, 'I live ... over there,' he says, waving his right arm vaguely towards his father's land.

'Oh, on one of the farms,' says another of the girls.

'Yes, that's right,' Adam answers swiftly, before Cedric gets them in to deeper water, 'and I live in Hardwick Road, overlooking the fields.'

'Now I know you're having us on,' says the tall girl, 'there's no Hardwick Road in Sedgefield.'

'Maybe not in your day, but there is now,' says Cedric, enjoying being one up on the girls. With a little nod to his mate and a slight smirk, he adds, 'You'd better tell them, Adam.'

Smiling broadly, more in surprise than amusement, Adam coughs lightly. 'Right, ....,' he starts, taking his mobile from his pocket. 'You won't have seen one of these before, but does Sedgefield have telephones yet ?'

The tallest girl tuts loudly and tells him, 'Well, we do, of course, my Dad has one in the shop, for the orders. Doesn't look like that though,' she says, pointing at the mobile.

'Well, everybody has these now, even kids, can't live without them,' says Adam, holding up his phone. 'Called a mobile, cos you can carry it about with you. But, this one is a bit special. Has magic powers, brought me and Cedric here across time. Back for me, forward for him.'

The girls, silent for once, gaze open-mouthed.

'Take your photo, as well, if you like.' Adam is really enjoying himself now, showing off. 'Come on,' he says. 'Line up, littlest one in the middle, that's right. Now smile.'

'Cheese !' the girls shout, much to Cedric's surprise. Screaming with laughter, they drag him into the line-up. 'Watch the birdie !' yells one of the girls, as Adam takes a second shot.

'And that's not all,' adds Cedric, wriggling away from the grasp of the group. Safely back by Adam's side, he proudly tells them, 'It can read strange tongues and make us invisible.'

'What do you mean invisible ?' says the smallest girl, glancing to her friend for support. 'We can see you.'

'Aye,' says her taller pal, 'large as life and twice as

ugly.' All three girls laugh, a bit nervous now. They don't know what to make of these two strangers and their tall tales.

'Less your cheek,' says Cedric, growing in confidence by the minute. 'You should think yourselves lucky. Only certain people can see us.'

'Pull the other one,' says the tallest girl, 'You must think we were born yesterday.'

'As a matter of interest, when were you born ?' asks Adam, keen to know what time zone they've landed in now. Cedric adds, 'Seeing as we're all the same age.'

'1933, seeing as you're asking,' says the cheeky one, pointing first to herself, then to each of her friends in turn. ' I'm Joan, that's Norma with the fair hair and the little one's Lily.'

'So, it must be 1945,' says Adam, looking to Cedric for support.

'Oh, well done,' says Joan, 'He can add up an'all.'

'Not just a pretty face,' says Norma, setting them all off giggling again.

'Wartime,' Adam explains to Cedric, looking around for barbed wire, army jeeps, blackout curtains. Signs of war on the home front he'd seen on films and in books at school.

'That's right,' Norma steps forward from her two friends. 'That's why I'm here. I come from Newcassel, but there was a lot of bombing going on up there, cos of the docks and that, so I was evacuated to Sedgefield.'

'There's a few vaccys,' adds Joan, keen to show off her local knowledge  in front of visitors. 'The three Donnelly lads, they're staying with the Pavitts over at the kennels by Hardwick Park. And the Greenwell brothers, they're with Aggie Bell, the verger, helps out in church,  you know.'

Adam tells Cedric, 'A lot of kids were sent away from home during the war. For safety. Must have been awful.'

'Not for me it isn't,' says Norma brightly,' I love it here, we all do, all my family. In fact, when the war finishes, we're planning on stopping here, if we can.'

'Anyway, me mam says you'd never know there was a war on in Sedgefield,' says Lily.'Well, apart from the air

raid shelter on the green and the army camp down Durham Road.'

'I've heard about that before,' says Adam. 'I'd like to get a peek in there sometime, Cedric.'

Joan takes charge again. 'Anyway, you're stopping our game. We were playing itchy dabber when you landed and it's my go.'

'No it's not, it's mine,' Lily speaks up, smiling. 'Just 'cos it's your dad's shop you think you own the pavement.' Taking the little empty shoe polish tin from her friend, she bends her knees, takes her right hand back and gently slides the marker over the numbered squares.

'A four ! Great ! That's more like it.' Placing a foot on the first square, chalked with a big number one, she balances carefully, both arms out to steady herself. 'Now then,' she says, quietly, almost to herself, 'watch the expert.' Away she hops, tongue sticking out to one side of her mouth for added concentration.  Balancing on One, hopping on to Two, knee up for Three, hop to four. Pick up the tin. Jump and turn. Feet apart on Four, Five, ready to go back.

'J-o-o-oh - nee ! Come on, get yourself in here. It's nearly ready and they won't want it cold.' A sudden voice from inside the shop stops Lily in her tracks.

'All right, Mam, won't be a minute.' Joan explains to the lads, 'Every week she makes a big pan of broth for the old folks at the almshouses. I have to go with her, help  her dish it up.'

Lily carries on, hopping all the way back to number one. Norma is just about to take her turn at itchy dabber, when a man's voice booms out of the shop.

'Come on, our Joan, didn't you hear your mother ? I've told you before about playing there. It stops the customers getting in and they can't see what I've got in the window.' Butcher Davison stands in the shop doorway, arms folded over his paunch, hair slicked down with Brylcreem, his long white apron smeared with blood. 'You lasses can get that rubbed out, an' all. Makes the place look untidy.' Without a backward glance, he stomps back inside, not even noticing the two lads standing stock still on his precious pavement.

'Looks like it's still working, Cedric,' mutters Adam, as Lily and Norma start scuffing at the pavement, the rubber soles of their plimsolls making short work of the numbers they'd chalked so carefully. 'Rightoh, Mr Davison,' they chorus obediently, only sniggering when Joan's Dad is well out of earshot. Joan, not usually lost for words, stands staring at the space where her father has just been.

'That magic oojamaflip must do like you say, make you invisible. He never saw you. Me Dad always chases the lads away from the shop. Doesn't like them hanging round.'

'Except for Billy Cooper,' says Lily, shyly. 'He's the butcher lad, delivers meat on his bike.'

Cedric, busy watching the girls show them how to play itchy dabber, had forgotten all about the sides of meat hanging in the window. And, of course, he has no idea what a bike is. But, by now, he's quite at home with Adam's magic mobile and its impressive powers.

'It seems that only certain people are able to see us. Those who have passed twelve summers on this green earth. To the rest, we are invisible.' Pleased with his simple explanation, Cedric smiles broadly, proud to share the mysteries of the mobile with yet more new friends.

'Don't you talk funny ?' Lily blushes slightly at her own boldness, linking her arm through her friend's for confidence.

'Divvent worry, man, Cedric.' Norma smiles kindly. 'They used to say that about me when I first landed from Newcassel. They soon got used to us.'

Rubbing out the last few lines of their game, she says, 'Right, Lily, we'd better get off before we get wrong again off Joan's dad.'

'See you later, girls,' says Joan, 'I'll get my pocket money after I've done the broth. We'll mebbe go to Maggie Bell's for some bull's eyes.'

'They're sweets,' Adam explains quickly as Cedric looks horrified. 'Made with sugar and stuff, you know.' Not much wiser, but pleased to know they can't be found in the butcher's window, Cedric shrugs and smiles.

'Nice meeting you, boys,' says Lily, still clinging to Norma's arm. 'You're nothing like the lads round here at all.'

Norma shakes her head in agreement. 'And that mobile doo-dah teks some beatin' an'all. Mind you send us a copy of the snaps.' As they set off to walk away, Norma looks back over her shoulder. 'Tara lads,' she calls with a smile.
'Tara,' adds Lily with a giggle, 'Drop in again soon.'

With a final wave, the two girls wander off up the street, arm in arm.

The smell of broth wafts through the shop, as Joan's mam carries the big black metal pan through from the hob. Still piping hot, steam creeps out from under the lid, the earthy scent of good dark meat and rich gravy filling the air. Mrs Davison's face glows red with the effort of her morning's work. Two thick cloths save her hands from the heat, one round the hooped handle, the other underneath, her hand steadying the heavy pot.

'It smells lovely, Mam,' says Joan, enjoying the sharp tang of the weekly broth.

Balancing the pot on the end of the shop counter, her mam tucks a stray lock of hair back inside the old-fashioned mob cap she always wore to do the cooking. Wiping her hands on her blue patterned wrap-around pinny, 'So it should,' she says. 'Good scrag end of neck in there, plenty fresh vegetables, a cupful of barley and a good sprinkling of salt and pepper.'

His nose tingling at the lovely smell, Cedric grabs his stomach as it gives a loud rumble. Adam stifles a laugh. Joan tries to pretend they're not there.

Unaware of the two lads, Mrs Davison unhooks the metal ladle hanging from a hook under the counter and hands it to Joan.

'There you are, honey, I'll hold the pot, you can dish it out. Come on now, let's get a move on.  Cos you know what old Billy always says if we're late.'

Smiling, they carry the big pot between them, Joan conducting with the ladle, as she and her mam shout out in chorus, ' 'bout time ! Me belly thinks me throat's cut !'

'Well,' says Adam after a moment, 'that's all we're going to get, a sniff of the broth pan.'

'Reminds me of the stew my mother makes,' Cedric looks longingly up the street. 'Only ours has more veg, less meat.'

Following at a safe distance, the two lads take a closer look at the almshouses.  A row of ten little houses, with a sharp pitched roof and five pairs of tall thin chimneys. Ten tiny windows, but only five little doors, the middle one topped with a fancy arch and a narrow pointed roof. A shield set into the brickwork bears a carved ribbon and the words Cooper's Almshouses. 'Brilliant,' says Adam, taking a photo.

'That shield's in the church wall now, Ced, near the ball game sculpture.' He clicks another shot. 'It's great to see the almshouses in the flesh. By my day, they're just a memory on the history trail. Built in 1703, supposed to last for ever. Knocked down before I was born.'

'Surprise, surprise,' whispers Cedric, 'You'd better not tell Joan. She'll be out of a job.'

His stomach rumbles loudly again, the aroma of butcher's broth now a memory too.

'I know, Cedric, I'm starving as well. I could kill an Indian.' Laughing at the shocked look on his pal's face, Adam explains. 'Takeaway, Indian takeaway. Or a pizza, you'd like them, mate. Better than a window full of raw meat any day. '

'Why don't you whizz us forward then ?' says Cedric. 'See if we can land back in your time.'

'Good idea,' Adam agrees, pulling his mobile from his shorts' pocket. '2-0-1-5 again?'

The lads smile as they both chorus their favourite catch phrase – 'Worth a try !'

# MAY THIS GAME BE BETTER THAN THE LAST

'Da – dah !' cries Adam as they land, much more gently this time. He holds out his right arm in a grand gesture towards the place where the pizza shop should be.

'One of these days,' says Cedric, picking himself up off the wet grass, 'one of these days, you'll land us in the right spot.'

'We're in the right spot,' protests Adam. 'Well, more or less. Just not the right time.'

'Even I can see that,' says Cedric, 'No ... pizza ... then,' he sighs. 'Fraid not, mate.'

As they look around, the boys slowly realise that they haven't moved far from the almshouses they left in 1945.

''I don't recall that big place from last time,' says Cedric, looking up at a square building sitting at the end of the little row of almshouses. Two floors high, with three big windows on each level and a group of three chimneys on top.

'I bet that's the old school,' says Adam, 'Massive isn't it ? That bottom part was a prison once over. All gone by my day.'

'You don't say,' smiles Cedric. 'Lucky the church is still standing.'

St. Edmund's still towers above the village green. No lych gate, though. Just a gap in the wall running along in front of the church.  No war memorial either.

'Must be before the Great War then,' says Adam. '1914 - 18, Cedric, the war to end all wars.'

Looking a bit puzzled and dropping easily into his new pal's way of talking, Cedric says, 'Hang on. Didn't you say it was wartime the last time we landed ?'

'Different war, Ced.  Well done, you're learning fast.' Adam explains, 'World War II. Started 1939. Nearly over by the time we were talking to the lasses. VE Day May 1945.' Taking another look around, he adds, 'We've gone back in time, but don't ask me how far.'

'This lad might be able to tell us,' Cedric nods towards a stout boy walking across the green, a huge chunk of bread in his hand. Several other people, mostly adults, have walked straight past the two lads without a second glance. Not this one, though.

'Now then, lads, all right, ready for the game ?' Taking another bite from the wedge of bread, he wipes the back of his hand across his mouth. Both boys look on, longingly.

'Have you had no breakfast, lads ? Oh sorry, here's me wolfing this down.' Reaching into the pocket of his thick wool trousers, the plump lad drags out another enormous piece of bread and dripping. 'I was saving it for after, but go on, split that atween you.'

With a quick 'Thanks, mate', Adam grabs the bread, tears it roughly in two and hands half to Cedric. Not a word is said for a long moment, while all three boys enjoy the simple food – thick soft bread covered in honey coloured fat. Salty with flecks of brown sweetness from tiny scraps of meat. Finishing his breakfast, the plump lad wipes his hands down the legs of his trousers. 'Bread and drip, can't beat it for building you up. Like our James says, you need muscles for this game, kidder. I'm Johnny, by the way, James is me big brother.'

'Pleased to meet you,' says
Adam, rubbing his hands on
his shorts before shaking
Johnny's greasy hand.
'I'm Adam, he's Cedric.
Thanks for the breakfast,
we were starving.'
Licking the last crumbs
of bread from his lips,
Cedric rubs his now
silent stomach.
Smiling, he says,
'Best meal I've had in
ages. Now, Johnny, you say
there's a game today ?'

'It'll be the ball game, is it ?
Adam jumps in. 'Shrove
Tuesday Ball Game. It's mint !'

Puzzled by Adam's turn of
phrase, Johnny says,
'Don't know about mint.
I know it's fast and hard
and sometimes
bones get broken.

Been going on for hundreds of years.'

'I got a kick of the ball this year, first time ever,' says Adam. 'Half term, so we could come down without nicking off.'

'What do you mean, this year ?' asks Johnny, 'We haven't had it yet. It's on today.'

'Oh right ..., when I say this year, I don't mean ...  this year ... now. I mean 2015.'

'What you on about, 2015 ? This year ? This year's 18 hundred and 80, mate.'

'A hundred years on from our Hardwick visit,' cries Adam. Johnny looks from one boy to the other, mystified.

'Can I explain this time ?' asks Cedric boldly, feeling quite at ease after his earlier trips.

'Go on then,' agrees Adam, handing him the mobile.

'See, Johnny, like he says, Adam is from 2015. I'm from about a thousand years earlier and this little box lets us travel about in time. Clever isn't it ?' Cedric beams with pride.

Johnny laughs quietly in disbelief. 'Just round

Sedgefield though,' adds Adam.

'Or Ceddesfeld as it's called in my day,' says Cedric. 'After my father, you know.'

'Oh aye,' sniggers Johnny, 'Who's he when he's at home ? Lord of the manor or summat.'

'And there's more,' grins Adam, 'I wouldn't mind betting you're twelve years old.'

'You're right, I've just left school, thank goodness,' Johnny points to the big square building. 'That's it over there, used to be a prison. Still is, if you ask me.'

'Thought as much,' says Adam, 'that's why you can see us and all these other folks can't.'

'We're invisible,' crows Cedric proudly, 'to all those who are not just twelve summers old.'

As the boys are talking, young lads and older men start gathering, wandering up the street in twos and threes. Warmly dressed like Johnny in thick wool trousers, collarless shirts and dark jackets, their heavy leather boots clatter on the hard road as they stride towards the green.

'When I first saw the pair of you I thought you looked a

bit odd, you know, your clothes and that,' grins Johnny. 'Mind, we get all sorts turning up for the ball game. Lasses as well.'

'You might get away with it then, Cedric,' Adam nudges his new mate, 'with your tunic and long hair, anybody who spots you will think you're a girl.' Adam and Johnny burst out laughing, but Cedric is more than a match for them by now. Calmly looking round at the groups gathered on the green, he quietly says, 'I reckon I'll be all right. You too, Adam.'

The others stop laughing, surprised for a moment by Cedric's manner, wise beyond his years.

'It seems to me there must be some other folks around here the same age as you, Johnny.'

'Oh aye,' Johnny answers, 'Nobody likes to miss the ball game.'

'Well, as none of them seem to have spotted us, not even me in my frock,' Cedric goes on, putting a sarcastic stress on that last word, 'I guess you alone can see us, Johnny.'

'You reckon ?' says Johnny, rather pleased to have exclusive access to these two strange visitors. 'Does that mean I'm invisible an'all ?'

'Doubt it,' smiles Adam, linking arms with his old pal. 'It just means everyone'll think you're talking to yourself.' Looking sharply round to see if anyone is watching, Johnny shoves his hands into his pockets. Eyes darting to left and right, his mouth pushed out into a round O, he starts a tuneless whistle. He falls silent as another young lad yells across to him.

'How do, Johnny, all reet ?' Flinging his arms round the shoulders of two other lads, he dashes across the green, dragging them along protesting on either side. 'Gi'ower, man Tommy,' yells one, trying to wriggle out of his mate's grasp. 'Pack in, you daft ha'porth !'

The other breaks free with a friendly shove.

'Old school pals,' Johnny mutters through clenched teeth. 'Say nowt, Cedric,' whispers Adam, as the three come to a halt in front of them. 'All right mate, had your pancakes yet ?

As still as statues either side of Johnny, Adam and Cedric hold their breath. Much as they would like to chat to these lads, they don't fancy trying to explain themselves all over again. 'No, not yet, Tom, you know me mother always makes us wait for the twelve o'clock bell.' The other two lads, more interested in shoving each other about and practising their shin-kicking skills, don't bother to speak. Wanting to test out his invisibility, Adam tries to attract their attention. Putting his thumbs on either side of his head and waving his fingers, he sticks his tongue out and crosses his eyes. Johnny looks panic stricken. These are hard lads. Punch first, run fast. But they don't seem to notice.

'How about you, Tom ?' says Johnny, stepping in front of Adam and throwing a warning glance at Cedric. 'Had your pancakes yet ? Ready for the game ?'

'No, not yet,' says Tommy, still taking no notice of Johnny's two side-kicks. 'Just out for a wander with these two clowns. Better be getting back. Not many minutes to the noonday bell.'

He heads back over the green, his two mates, still kicking and punching each other, following behind like a couple of snapping dogs. Johnny watches, Adam and Cedric either side of him, all three silent until Tommy and his side-kicks are well away.

'Mad them two,' says Johnny after a while. 'Marky and Seth, always in trouble at school. Tom's all right, but they're crackers.'

'Are they brothers ?' asks Cedric, glad to be able to move and breathe again.

'Why, no,' says Johnny, 'Just mates, same as me, all the same age.'

'Twelve !' all three chorus. 'But they couldn't see us,' grins Adam.

'Just as well,' says Cedric, 'with you mucking on like that.'

'Aye,' Johnny agrees, 'you could have ended up with a black eye.' Looking up at the church tower, he says, 'Any road, I'd better be getting back an'all. Don't want to miss the pancake bell. Tell you what, why don't you two come with us ?'

Adam and Cedric perk up no end at the prospect of more food, after going without for so long. 'Sounds good to me,' says Adam, 'As long as we don't get you into any bother, Johnny.'

'I eat that many pancakes,' he says, grinning, 'me Ma'll never notice if I slip you two the odd one.'

He sets off towards his house, just beyond the village green, only a short walk from the church. The other two scurry after him, hidden to all eyes but those of their new mate.

'I'll have to watch out for our James, that's all. Me brother. Fifteen he is, thinks he can boss us about. I have to share a bedroom with him, worse luck. His snoring's enough to rattle the tiles on the roof, his feet stink and he farts like a field full of sheep.'

The other two lads laugh out loud. 'I know what that can be like,' smiles Cedric.

'Then there's me little sister, our Daisy, she's canny enough. She'll be helping me mam with the pancakes. Only ten, but ample old enough to be learning how to cook. I mean, she'll have to do it when she's married, won't she ? You'll not catch a Sedgefield man making his own dinner. Me Pa's never so much as washed a pot. Women's work, he says.'

'He wouldn't get away with that in my day,' smiles Adam, 'I can just see my Mam waiting hand and foot on my Dad – not !'

They soon reach Johnny's house and step straight in to the kitchen. In the corner, a dark wooden fireplace surrounds the family stove, black leaded every day.  A copper kettle blackened with years of service sits on glowing coals. The central fire throws out heat to two ovens, one on each side. The main one, on the left, squat and solid, the other narrower. In front of it, a flat iron tipped on its handle, not needed just now.

'Just in time, me lad,' says his mother, shoving up her sleeves. She loops her big white apron over her head, reaching the long narrow tapes round her waist and back again to tie in front.

'Right, let's get cracking. Pass us that big mixing bowl, son.' Johnny reaches the earthenware dish down from the shelf. 'Now then, Daisy, you've seen me make pancakes often enough, 'bout time you had a go.'

Johnny and his two pals stand back out of the way while Daisy and her mother set to work.

'Right, honey,' Ma passes Daisy a large round flour jar.' Take the top off, aye. Now tip it up gently, till you've just got the right amount in your bowl.'

With both hands wrapped tight round the heavy jar, Daisy gives a couple of nervous shakes, flecks of flour flying up in to her face. She plops the jar back on to the big wooden table, wiping her brow with the back of her hand. A pinch of salt from the jar by the fire, then Daisy digs her hands in the flour, pushing it up against the sides of the big bowl to make a well in the middle. She cracks three eggs into a brown jug, beating them up into a deep yellow foam.

'From our own hens this morning, couldn't be fresher,' Johnny quietly tells his new mates.

'That's right, son,' says his mother, totally unaware of the two visitors. Cedric and Adam give each other the thumbs up, sure now that only Johnny knows they're there.

'Good lass, Daisy, you're doing a grand job,' Ma smiles. Beaming back, the little girl lifts the jug and pours the eggy mixture into the well of the flour, mixing it in with a wooden spoon. Then some milk with a tiny bit of water added.

'Makes all the difference that,' says Ma. 'That drop water keeps the mix nice and light. Now take it steady, Daisy, you don't want to beat the livin' daylights out of it.'

Using a metal spoon now, Daisy makes swooping figures of eight, her wrist turning and turning like a skater on a pond.

'That's it, pet, round and round you go, gently does it, until all the flour's mixed in.'

Once finished to mother's satisfaction, Daisy covers the pancake mixture with a clean cloth.

'I'll put it near the window where it's cool, Ma, while we wait for the noon day bell.'

Only a few minutes later, the church bell tolls the first of twelve slow bongs. Ma drops a lump of white fat into the frying pan, set to warm on top of the main oven. With a hissing sizzle, the fat slides around the hot pan, its black surface soon covered in a golden sheen.

The bell still tolls as the front door bursts open and Johnny's father and brother land home.

'Howay Ma, I'm clammin' ,' says James, grabbing a seat. 'Bags I first one out the pan.'

'Less your lip, our James.' His father pulls up a chair to the big table. 'Get sat down and wait your turn. You know your mother always gets first one, being the cook.'

'Should be our Daisy today then, by rights.' says her Ma, proudly. 'She's done all the work.'

Johnny takes his place at the table, as far away as he can get from his father and brother.

'What's up with you, lad ? Do I pong or summat ?' James sniffs around his own armpits.

'No worse than usual,' Johnny snaps back, shuffling around on his seat.

'That's enough.' Ma flips the first pancake. 'If you don't shurrup, you'll get none, ball game or no ball game.'

His shoulders hunched and head down, Johnny swivels round in his chair to where the two lads are standing. He needs them to get nearer to him and out of sight, so he can sneak a pancake or two under the table. Pancakes floating in the air might just arouse suspicion. Johnny daren't speak. He lifts his head, looks straight at the two lads, invisible in the corner, and nods towards the floor.

'There you are, Pa, first one for you.' Daisy carefully puts a plate in front of her father. She walks round the table. 'And one for our James.' As all eyes are now on the pancakes, the two lads take their chance to dart down under the table. Crouched there, silent and very hungry, they don't have long to wait before a pancake appears, hidden in Johnny's curled hand. Adam breaks it in two and the lads gobble up their share in seconds. Within moments, another arrives, then another.

'By, you're getting through them faster than ever, our Johnny,' says his mother.

'Oh, you know me, Ma. I love me pancakes,' Johnny grins, pleased that he's managed to share the feast with his invisible pals under the table.

Licking his lips, rubbing his great hands together, then wiping his mouth, Pa says, 'Well done, our Daisy. Them pancakes were nearly as good as your mother's.' The little wooden chair screeches against the stone floor as he pushes it back and stands up from the table. 'Now, about time we set off for the game.'

Adam and Cedric scramble out from their hiding place under the table. They fall into step behind Johnny, following his Pa and brother James. Only a short walk from their house to St Edmund's. Crowds gathering now on Cross Hill in front of the church. Huddled groups of lads, older men who've seen it all before, a few girls, some hoping for a kick at the ball, most ready to scream and run if the game comes anywhere near them.

'Now then lads, how're you doing ? Got your leg

guards on ?' A stout, red faced lad yells at them across the green. As he comes closer, Adam and Cedric are pleased to see that he's not talking to them. Just the other two lads. Pa has joined a group of his own pals nearby.

'Why, no, Fred, man,' James laughs, 'what d'ye take me for ? Some soft townie ?'

'Aye, well, don't blame me if you get hurt. There'll be plenty shin kickin' the day.'

'I'll be all right, don't worry, mate.' He turns to his brother, elbowing him in the ribs.

'Mind, you'd better keep out the road, our Johnny. Me Ma'll kill us if I take you home with owt brocken.' The two older lads have a good laugh at the young one's expense.

'Gi' ower. I can look after mesel'. I'll be having a kick of the ball, don't you fear.' Cedric and Adam nod invisible encouragement at their new pal.

'Don't fret, pet. I'll pick the ball up and let you have a touch of it.' James ruffles Johnny's hair, laughing, egging Fred on to join in, making fun of the younger lad.

'Leave him alone !' Pa shouts across to shut the pair of them up. Walking back to his sons, he puts an arm round Johnny's shoulder. 'You stick wi' me, son. We'll get plenty of sport, din't worry. Hey up, there's the rector, d'ye see him ?  Sooner him than me climbing all them steps.'

Tipping their heads back, Adam and Cedric peer up at the church tower, grey against the steely blue of the sky. Squinting in the hazy sun, they can just make out the stark black of the priest's cassock and cloak, in sharp contrast with the ancient stones around him.

'Welcome everyone,' he calls down to the crowd. 'God's blessings on you this fine Shrove Tuesday. I wish you good sport. As the rhyme has it, may this game be better than the last !'

The church bell rings once as he flings the ball out in to the crowd. A great cheer goes up, everyone surges forward. Swarming like honey bees, men and boys weave back and forth, all trying for a touch of the ball. One minute it's bowling along the ground, dribbled and kicked by any foot that can reach. The next, speeding away, soon swallowed up by a scrummage of legs and boots.

Rooted to the spot, Cedric watches entranced by the crowd, the noise, the excitement.

'I've never seen so many people before,' he says, almost to himself.

Busy watching the to and fro of the game, Pa doesn't even notice Johnny talking to the fresh air. 'There's always a crowd turns up on Ball Game Day,' he quietly tells his two new pals. 'Town and Country, see, them's the two teams.'

'No teams in my day,' says Adam, 'it's every man for himself.'

Then, before Johnny can think, there's the ball, right at his feet. How did it get there? Never mind, just kick it ! A great stupid smile spreads over his face as the ball flies off, back in to the fray. His two invisible pals grab each other, jumping and yelling for all they're worth.

'I did, it Pa, I did, I got a kick at the ball !' Breathless with excitement, Johnny beams up into his father's face. Slapping him firmly on the back and shaking his youngest son's hand for the first time in Johnny's life, his Pa smiles broadly back. 'Well done, son, I'm proud of you. You can join the men now.' Adam takes his chance to snap a quick photo of the smiling pair.

'Does that mean I can come to the pub with you when the ball's won?' Johnny grins.

'Now don't go gettin' ahead of yourself.' Trying to look solemn, his father goes on. 'There's a good few hours of this game to go yet and a good few years before I'll be taking you to any pub. Right, I'm off to catch the ball up. I haven't had a kick mesel' yet.'

Off he runs, the clatter of his heavy boots echoing down the street. The three lads stick together as the crowd sweeps and swirls across the grass, more brown than green now, churned up by dozens of pairs of running feet. Adam grabs another pic as they fly past.

'Oh, you have to be on the ball, if you see what I mean,' laughs Adam. 'I only just managed to tap it myself before this great big fella picked it up and threw it across the road.'

'In your day, you mean ?' says Johnny, still watching the ball. 'No chucking allowed in my time.' All eyes fixed on the little brown ball hurtling back and forth, nobody takes any notice of one young lad who seems to be talking to himself. With a sudden surge, the crowd follows the ball as it changes direction, heading towards the top of the street.

'Oh, no,' shouts Johnny, as the roaring mob veer left, 'they're making for the Townie goal.'

The three lads start running, following the crowd, now heading out towards open country.

'If they get as far as the beck out by Foxton, we've had it.' Johnny pulls up, bending over, both hands on his knees, struggling for breath. ' Sorry, lads, can't keep up.'

'Must be all the pancakes,' grins Cedric, watching the ragged crowd disappearing into the distance.

'They're bound to head back this way in a minute,' says Adam, 'Nobody wants the game to finish too soon, no matter which side you're on, eh Johnny ?'

'You're right there, mind, but I'd sooner they were heading for our alley than theirs. Can't have the townies beating us country lads, can we, Cedric ?' His breath restored, Johnny stands up, his two hands pressed into his back for support. Just like his Pa after hard work.

Glad to be included in the team for this thrilling game he's only just discovered, Cedric asks, 'Where's our alley then, Johnny ? Over in the fields as well ?'

'Why, no,' says Johnny, 'You can nearly see it from

here. Just past the bend in the road, next to Issy Alderson's blacksmiths.' Stretching his right arm over Cedric's head, he points along North End, beyond the stately Manor House and the arched entrance to the Hardwick Arms.

'That's what we're aiming for, the country alley,' says Johnny, 'Only a muddy little pond, but worth fighting for.'

'So, once it lands in the water, your team's won ?' asks Cedric.

'No, no, it's not as simple as that,' says Johnny, keeping an eye out for the crowd coming back towards the village. 'Once the ball's had a good soaking, one of the team has to grab it back and run with it to the bull ring. Pass it through three times and that's it, game over. The winner gets to keep the ball for ever.' He leads the other two lads towards the all-important metal ring, set in to cobblestones on a patch of scruffy grass.

'Make a good photo that, Ced,' says Adam, handing him the mobile. Grinning with pride at being entrusted with the camera, Cedric ducks down to get a close-up of the goal. 'Now you two,' he says, organising Adam and Johnny either side of the bull ring. Leaning over, each pretending to have the ball, they grin up at Cedric as he clicks another memory for the gallery.

'In my day,' says Adam, as they stand up, 'the game starts like that as well, not from the church tower. One of the oldest villagers is picked, all in secret, comes along on the day, passes the ball through the ring three times, chucks it up and that's it. Game on ! Lasts for hours, cos the ball gets taken in to the pubs. And it usually goes out of the village in a car.'

Seeing the puzzled looks from both lads, Adam quickly explains, 'Like a horse and cart – without the horse. Everybody has them nowadays.'

'And pubs are where you go for a pint of beer, Cedric,' adds Johnny, helpfully, 'when you're old enough, like.'

'Not twelve summers, then,' grins Cedric. 'Pity, I like the sound of these pubs.'

'There's plenty of 'em in Sedgefield,' says Adam, nodding to The Black Lion in front of them. 'Then there's The Hardwick Arms over the road, the Hope down there opposite the church, the Dun Cow and the Golden Lion at the bottom...'

Cedric clicks away, as Adam points out each pub in turn, finishing with a grand sweep of his left arm towards the last one. ' ... and the Nag's Head round the corner.'

'Then there's the Black Bull, the Red Lion, the Buck Inn and Tenement House,' adds Johnny, counting them off on his fingers, until he's used them all up.

'Blimey,' says Adam, 'I thought we had a lot in my day, but you have even more.'

'Aye, well,' grins Johnny, 'as me Pa says, thirsty work farming.'

A great roaring shout and the clatter of working boots heralds the return of the battling crowd. Mobile at the ready, Cedric tries to catch some action shots, as the game speeds along. Rushing back towards the village, covered in mud from the soggy winter fields, lads and men scramble for a kick at the ball. Fearsome warriors, neither side ready to give in. At the front, Johnny's brother and his mate panting for breath, but running like hounds after a fox. Blood running from his forehead, dried to brown like the mud on his hands, James spots his brother watching from the Black Lion corner.

'Howay, man, Johnny,' he yells, his voice hoarse from the day's shouting, 'Divvent stand there like a drip. Get yersel ower 'ere with the men.'

Turning swiftly round towards his two new mates, invisible to all but him, Johnny mouths, 'See you later, lads.' Then he's off, dashing with the crowd towards the country alley. Cedric catches a final image of their fleeing backs.

# OFF TO THE ASYLUM

'Now we'll never know who won,' says Cedric, his mouth turned down at the corners with disappointment. Stopped in their tracks, breathless from running, the two lads gaze ahead, looking in vain for any sign of Johnny. Or the crowd. Or the game. The blacksmith's shop is still there in front of them, but no pond. 'They must have filled it in,' Adam whispers, trying to make sense of the change of scene. All the noise and excitement had stopped in an instant.

'Like switching off the telly,' says Adam, a slow smile spreading across his face. He swings round towards Cedric. 'Have you still got my mobile, mate ?'

'Of course,' says Cedric, holding out his hand, tightly clutched around the silver box. 'I never let go of it, Adam, not even in all that chasing about.'

'Good lad,' says Adam, taking the phone from him. 'I wonder if mebbe you pressed a number while you were clinging on to it, by mistake like.'

'Well I didn't mean to,' says Cedric, looking worried

now, 'I haven't broken it, have I ?'

'No, mate, no, don't worry,' Adam puts a friendly arm round Cedric's shoulder. 'I just think we might have found yet another string to this little beauty's bow.'

Cedric shakes his head, in the dark once again.

'You know,' says Adam, jigging about as he tries to explain, 'fiddle ... bow ... music.'

One or two people walk past the two lads chatting on the corner. Adam playing the air violin,  Cedric laughing his head off. Nobody takes the least bit of notice.

'This is the only way I can make music,' says Cedric, puckering up his lips and whistling a lively little tune.

'Very good, mate, but I don't think you're ready for X Factor.' Adam grins.

'Is that on the ... telly, by any chance ?' asks Cedric, waggling his head and smiling with delight at remembering the strange little word.

'You're dead right, there, pal,' says Adam, holding up the mobile. Waving it gently in his hand, he adds, 'and that's where this comes in.'

The two lads perch on a little low wall opposite the smithy while Adam explains.

'See, a mobile looks a bit like a remote for the telly. My Mam's always getting ours mixed up. She doesn't watch what she's doing, then she wonders why Eastenders doesn't come on.'

Listening intently, Cedric crunches up his forehead until wavy lines appear on his brow.

'When I get hold of it, I click through the channels, drives her mad.' Adam shakes his head, laughing. 'But that's the whole idea; you can change programmes at the push of a button.'

'And you think that's what I did ?' says Cedric, beginning to understand the new power of this marvellous machine.

'Aye, I do, mate,' Adam nods, 'but not just telly channels. You've changed time itself.'

'It was nothing,' says Cedric, beaming broadly. 'I wonder what year we've landed in now.'

'No idea, Ced, but I guess we're not too far away from your father's feld and his flock. See them ?' Adam points across to a pair of stone pillars, elaborate iron gates hanging between. 'Not there in my day. They must be the park gates I've heard about.'

'Hardwick Park ?' asks Cedric, jumping up to look across the fields. 'Where Jack works ? Pity we had to leave there in such a hurry.'

'Aye, well, that's time travel for you.' Adam grins as they wander back up the street towards the village. Little has changed since they met Johnny in 1880. The roadway is a bit better and there's a pavement to walk on now. Houses on the left, just before they reach the Black Lion corner, Burdon's Tailor and Draper shop, the window full of straw hats and gloves. Near the Hardwick Arms a horse stands patiently, the little wooden cart behind loaded with furniture.

A young girl darts out from the baker's opposite, a wicker basket over her arm.

'She might be able to give us a clue,' says Adam, 'looks about the right age.'

'Well there's only one way to find out,' says Cedric, stepping boldly out in front of the girl.

'Excuse me,' she says, a little flustered, but not afraid to stick up for herself. 'I'm in a hurry, please step aside.' Tightening her grip on the handle of her shopping basket, she takes a closer look at these two odd looking fellows.

'Forgive my friend,' says Adam, turning on the charm. 'He's not used to dealing with lovely ladies. Doesn't get out much.' Ignoring Cedric's sharp kick on the shin, Adam goes on. 'We're new in town and we were just wondering ... erm ... if you could help us out.'

With an impatient sigh and a shake of her head, the girl starts to walk away.

'You must be twelve years old,' barks Cedric, stopping her in her tracks. With a surprised frown, she looks back over her shoulder, 'How in the world do you know that ?'

'Because you can see us,' explains Cedric, matter of fact. 'To everyone else we're invisible.'

The girl laughs lightly, turning to face them. 'Just as well, looking like you do.' Her simple white pinafore over a dark blue skirt and plain blouse contrast sharply with Adam's denim shorts and Cedric's smock. 'Are you got up like that for a reason ?'

'Yeah,' snorts Adam, 'The reason being I've blown in here from 2015 and he's an Anglo Saxon.'

'Now, would you mind telling us what year we've

landed in ?' asks Cedric, all innocence.

'Nineteen hundred and eight,' the girl tells them, scratching her forehead and smiling in disbelief. 'You've come a long way.'

'Not really,' Adam explains seriously. 'We were last here for the ball game in 1880.'  'We've been all the way back to Roman times before now,' adds Cedric. 'This was just a short hop,' says Adam, tapping the phone safely tucked away in his jeans pocket. 'One click of the magic mobile and here we are.'

'Morning, Edith.' An old lady, her silver hair scraped back into a tight knot at the nape of her neck, stops for a word.  Dressed from top to toe in dusty black, clutching her basket in both hands, she nods towards the horse and cart. 'Nearly ready for flitting, I see.'

'That's right, Mrs March,' the girl replies nervously. 'Early start this morning. No breakfast even. Ma sent me out for a few bits of groceries, so we can have a bite when we get shifted.'

'Aye, well, best of luck, hinny.' Raising her left arm in farewell, the old lady crosses the street.  Edith and the lads watch in silence, until she disappears into the grocer's shop opposite. At last, they can breathe again.

'Now do you believe us ?' says Adam. 'That old biddy never saw us, did she ?'

With a quiet laugh, Edith shakes her head, still looking across at the shop doorway the old lady had clanged shut behind her. 'Doesn't look like it. Or I'd have had the sharp side of her tongue. Standing chatting to lads. She'd have been straight over the road to tell my Ma.'

'You're the chosen one this time' says Cedric solemnly. 'The first to set eyes on us who has lived for twelve summers.'

'Well I'm highly honoured,' smiles Edith, 'but I'll have to get on. My Ma'll be needing a helping hand. Not that we have much to shift, but it isn't easy with two little 'uns round your feet.'

She sets off over the road towards the place where the horse and cart are standing. The lads chase after her. Edith's their passport into Sedgefield 1908. They don't want to lose her so soon. Cedric gently strokes the horse's mane, while Adam, turning on his most winning smile, asks, 'So where are you moving to, Edith ? Not far from Sedgefield, I hope.'

'Just up the road to Winterton, the asylum' says Edith. 'My Pa works there. We're moving in to one of the cottages. A bit bigger than this one. I'll have my own bedroom at last.'

'Away from the two little 'uns ?' says Cedric, smoothing the rough brown coat of the docile horse harnessed to the loaded cart. He nods towards the window, where two mops of curly hair can just be seen above the sill, one dark, one fair. Edith smiles.

'Our Maggie and Mary, twins, six year old.  Like two china dogs on a mantel, Pa says. Ma  always has them dressed alike, but turn round twice and our Mary's as black as your hat, her hair sticking out like a stook of corn. Our Maggie stays neat as a pin, every curl in place.'

'That's why your Ma needs a hand,' says Adam, just as the front door opens.

'Come on our Edith, never mind standing talking to the hoss. I need you to keep an eye on these two blossoms, so I can give a hand with the packing.' She dashes back in again as quickly as she'd appeared, too busy to pause for breath.

'I'll have to go lads,' whispers Edith, with a final pat to the horse. 'Duty calls.'

'What a canny lass,' says Adam, as the door closes behind Edith. 'I wonder what becomes of her when the first war breaks out. She'll only be eighteen at the start. Old enough to work in munitions, though. For killing people, Cedric.'

As the lads stand pondering the young girl's fate, the front door of the little house opens. 'Now you keep an eye on the bairns, honey, while I get this on to the cart.' Edith's mother, small and stocky, lifts out an old brown suitcase, its lid held shut by two narrow leather belts, worn from years of use. Adam grabs Cedric's arm as he darts forward to lend a hand. The lads can do nothing but watch uselessly as the little woman drags the heavy load down the path. As she heaves the case up on to the back of the cart, they seize their chance. With a quick glance at each other, they dash up the path and in through the open door. Once inside the narrow front passage, they flatten themselves against the wall, holding their breath.

'Well, that's one more bit done.' Edith's mother steps back into the house, leaving the door open behind her. As she passes the little front room, she calls out, 'I hope you two are being good for your sister, mind.' Without waiting for an answer, she dashes on into the scullery at the back of the house.

'We are, Ma !' Two little heads peep out from the doorway. Standing behind them, Edith's jaw drops as she sees the two lads propped up against the wall. Both with silly grins on their faces. With a hand on each twin's shoulder, Edith takes a deep breath. Turning the girls away from the uninvited visitors, she says, brightly, 'Now, who wants another look at the horsey ?'

'Me, me, me !' both little girls shout, running back to their post at the window.

Spinning round to face the two lads, more surprised than angry, she hisses, 'What are you playing at ? Ma'll kill me if she sees you.'

'But she won't,' whispers Cedric, calmly. 'Nor your Pa, nor the little 'uns. Only you.'

'Can we stay a bit ?' asks Adam, smiling sweetly.

'Promise we'll be no trouble.'

'Edie ! Edie ! Come and lift us up !' One of the twins yells from the front room. Glancing towards the scullery where her mother is still busy packing, Edith makes a quick decision. 'All right then, but stay out of the way and, for goodness sake, keep quiet.'

Stepping in to the front room, Edith pulls the little stool up to the window, so the twins can stand on it to see out. 'Turns each,' she says, 'Come on, our Mary, you can go first. We don't want you screaming  blue murder if you have to wait.'

'Look ! Mr Mowbray's cart ! Doesn't our furniture look funny, Edie, all piled up like that ?'  Mary rubs the window glass, her plump little hand leaving smudges all over.  'Don't do that, Mary, you know mam's cleaned every inch of this house before we move.' Edith  lifts the little girl down, grumbling, before she can make any more mess.  'Not fair, our Edie, I want to stay up here.' Folding her arms tight round her middle, Mary sticks out her sulky bottom lip.

'You've had your go, come on, Maggie's turn now.' Holding on to her big sister's hand, the quieter little girl steps carefully on to the stool. Neither twin notices two lads sitting on the floor opposite the front window.

Watching, listening, but saying nothing.

'I'm a bit sad, aren't you, Edith ? We won't know anybody when we move.' Standing beside her, Edith puts a comforting arm round Maggie's waist.

'Well, I expect we'll miss our Sedgefield friends at first, but we're sure to make new ones. They say it's a massive place, Winterton, like another village really. I can't wait to see the farms and gardens. The patients grow all their own vegetables. They even keep pigs. They have their own church, St. Luke's, with a choir and an organ and everything.'

Maggie's little face looks a bit brighter now. 'I wonder if we'll go there to Sunday School,' she murmurs, gazing quietly out the window.

'Oh, Mary, look at the state of you.' A wooden tea chest packed full of pots and pans from  the scullery is left standing in the hallway while Mother pops in to check on the girls.

'I thought you were keeping an eye on them, Edith, not gawping out the window.'

Plonked down on the bare floorboards, every speck of dust mother missed had found its way on to Mary's face and her clean white pinafore. Edith shoots a quick glance at the boys, who must have seen it happen. They smile and shrug as if to say, 'You told us to keep out of the way and say nothing.'

Mother shouts back over her shoulder as she lugs the huge box out to the cart. 'Give her face a scrub and put a comb through her hair. She looks like she's been up the fireback.'

Mary smiles up at Edith like an angel, while her big sister spits on her hanky and gently rubs the dust from her face. She sings a little song to take Mary's mind off having her hair combed, usually sure to end in tears.

'Mary, Mary, quite contrary, how does your long hair grow? With curls and waves and ringlets too, no wonder we love you so !'

Maggie joins in, clapping along. 'Come on you two, let's get comfy.' They settle down either side of Edith on the clippy mat. She perches on the little fireside cracket, one of the few bits of furniture left in the front room.

'Tell us about our new house, Edith, where're we going to - Summerton, isn't it ?'

'No, you daft ha'porth,' Maggie chimes in, giggling, 'It's Winterton, you know that.'

'I hope it won't be cold all the time, then,' says Mary. 'There's a hole in my liberty bodice.' They all burst out laughing. The lads have a quiet smile, too, even though neither of them has a clue what a liberty bodice is. Then, remembering she's been trusted to look after her sisters like a proper grown-up, Edith becomes serious again.

'If you promise to sit still and not squirm about, our Mary, I'll tell you both all about it.'

'We promise !' they chorus, so Edith makes a start, putting on a real school marm voice.

'Well, children,' she says, 'Winterton's proper name is Durham County Asylum. Took nearly four million bricks to build it and it cost nearly £17,000.'

'Cripes,' says Maggie, her eyes wide with surprise, 'That's a lot of pennies.'

'How do you know, our Edith ? Who told you that ?' Mary's always full of questions.

'Father told me, ' says Edith, as sternly as she can.

'He says Robert Smith, who started it fifty years ago, had new ideas about how to look after lunatics.'

'What's lunatics ?' Mary butts in again.

Mother comes in just at that moment to collect the aspidistra in its large china pot from a tall table near the window. Placing the plant carefully on the floor, she quietly explains.

'They're people who are not very well in the head, children. Poor souls who just need a bit of help and somewhere quiet and pleasant to live so they can get better.'

With a kindly smile to all of her girls, she bustles back out to the removal cart, her pot and plant safely wrapped in a piece of sacking. The two lads share another glance. They're learning a lot, sitting here, saying nothing. Maggie's big blue eyes gaze up at her sister.

'Tell us some more, Edie. That Mr Smith, you said about, is he the man in charge ?

'That's right,' says Edith, cuddling them in again, 'Doctor Robert Smith. I've seen a picture of him. He looks terrifying with his big black beard and walking cane, but they say he's very kind. He thinks it'll do people good to be out in the fresh air, gardening and farming.'

'I'd like that,' Maggie says with a smile.'Do you think I'll be able to work on the farm, too ?'

'Course not,' jeers Mary, 'You have to be daft in the head, mother says.'

'MARY !' Both Edith and Maggie yell, shocked at their sister's blunt words.

'You're not to say that,' her quieter twin calmly puts Mary right. 'Mother said we have to be kind to them, poor souls.'

Her lip trembling again, knowing she's in the wrong but refusing to admit it, Mary mumbles, ' I know ... I didn't mean ...'

Just in the nick of time, Father comes through from the kitchen, carrying the old poss tub and dolly stick from out the backyard, the tin bath from the nail on the wall in his other hand.

'We'll still need these where we're going, girls. After all, like your Ma tells us, cleanliness is next to godliness.' He grins. The girls know this is one of their Ma's favourite sayings from the china plaques on display around the house. All carefully wrapped in newspaper now, packed away ready for the new cottage.

'Now, then, Edith, I hope these two cherubs are behaving themselves for you.'

'Good as gold.' She nods, smiling at her two little charges. Adam and Cedric exchange a glance, happy to share in Edith's little white lie. Cross legged on the clippy mat, heads tipped back, the twins gaze up at their Pa. Always the bolder, Mary pipes up.

'Our Edie's telling us all about Winterton, Pa.'

'The gardens and the farms,' adds Maggie, barely a beat behind her sister.

'Oh aye, they're grand.' Putting down his burdens for a moment, Father takes two minutes out from his removal jobs. 'Greenhouses, too, big fat tomatoes, lovely they are, fresh picked. The patients do all sorts of other work  too, you know. Some of the men make and mend shoes in the cobbler's shop. They do tailoring as well, jackets and trousers, like my best Sunday suit.'

He's just getting into his stride, when a shrill whistle from the carter outside reminds him of the job in hand.

'All right, man, I'm on me way. No rest for the wicked, eh girls ?'

Propping open the front door with one of mother's flat irons, he gathers up the poss tub and tin bath and heads outside for the cart.

'Do ladies live at Winterton, as well ?' asks Maggie, thoughtfully, as the front door bangs.

'Oh, yes,' Edith tells her, 'Mother says they have a sewing room, where they make all sorts - curtains, pillowcases, tablecloths, shirts, nightgowns, aprons. They even make shrouds to wrap dead bodies in !'

'Ooh, spooky !' Mary lifts up her arms, floating around the room. 'I bet there's a ghost as well.' Really enjoying herself now, Mary would have been even happier if she could have seen the two visitors grinning away at her antics in the corner.

'Edith, tell her !' Maggie clings to Edith, terrified, even though she knows it's only Mary making game. 'Don't like it !'

'Come on, lasses.' Mother pops her head in the front door. 'Nearly time for the off.  Good lass, Edith, you've been a grand little help while we've been loading up.'

Edith blushes to her roots. She's not used to being in charge and she knows pride's a sin. But she can't help feeling proud of herself, just this once. She's even managed to keep two unruly lads in their place.

'Now, pet, can you carry the cracket out to the cart, while I fetch the little table ?'

As Edith bends down to pick up the stool, Mary pipes up.

'We can help, too, Ma. Me and Maggie can carry the rug.'

'There's good girls.' Mother smiles as, one each end, they carefully carry out the clippy mat, hand-made beside the fire last winter. As precious as a storybook magic carpet. Unseen by all but Edith, the two lads slip out the front door. Mother picks up the tall narrow table from beside the window. Stepping out into the hallway, she spots father's make-shift doorstop.

'Well, Albert,' she laughs, 'We'd look a bit sick and scruffy without this.'

Picking up the flat iron, she slams the door on their old house. Placing the last tiny bit of furniture on the over-laden cart, mother takes her place on the wooden bench at the front, next to her husband. At the back of the cart, their legs dangling over the edge, Edith sits between the twins, one arm round each of them.

'Giddup !' says the driver, flicking the reins. With a little scream of delight as the cart sets off, the twins wave one arm each to their friends gathered in the road.

Only Edith can see two broadly grinning lads, four arms above their heads, eagerly waving back.

'Say cheese !' yells Adam, holding high his mobile to catch a parting shot of the smiling girls as they head off to their new home.

# LUCKY TO HAVE A PENNY

'Gotcha !' shouts Adam, as the girls disappear. Not just out of sight. Totally. Cart, horse, furniture, everything.

'Done it again, haven't you ?' A cheeky grin splitting his face, Cedric gazes up at his modern mate.

'Looks like it, Ced.' Adam smiles back. 'Just like me Mam and her remote. Missed Eastenders again.' Tucking the magic mobile back into his pocket, he shrugs. 'Never worry. Let's have a wander. See where we've landed up now.'

'Don't you mean when ?' says Cedric, looking round. 'We haven't moved from this spot.'

Sure enough, the boys are still standing in front of Edith's old house, looking along the road that leads to Winterton.

'Penny a long ride ! Penny a long ride !'

Plodding steadily towards them, heading for the centre of the village, two heavy horses, their heads bobbing in unison, pull a rickety old wooden cart. Two huge wheels at the back, two smaller ones in front, and on top a big rowing boat, painted in red, white and blue stripes. Across the bottom, a notice reads 'All children insured on this boat' and, carefully picked out in black shiny letters on either side 'Shamrock'. Turning left at The Black Lion Inn, the cart makes its way slowly down Front Street.

Keeping up his call 'Penny a long ride!  Penny a long ride !', the driver looks dressed for winter on this fine spring day. Blackened bony hands wearing fingerless gloves stick out from the sleeves of his dusty brown workman's coat. His back bent, he leans forward, gently clicking the horses' reins. Tipped low over his forehead, a battered old hat jammed on to his mass of wiry grey hair hides most of his face from view.

'Howay, Paddy, gis a smile.' The older lads guffaw as one of their gang cracks his annual joke.

'Less your lip, me lad,' growls the Shamrock man, 'or you'll not be gerrin' a go.'

'Hey, this looks like good fun.' Adam grins at Cedric, as they join the gathering crowd of kids running along behind his cart. 'I'll have to get a photo.' Nobody takes any notice of the two strangers until a girl nearby spots the mobile. Saying nothing at first, she looks

Cedric up and down, pointing her thumb towards Adam as if to say, 'What's he up to ?'

Nudging his mate, Cedric nods his head sideways towards the girl. After a quick click of his mobile, Adam looks across at her.

'I think we've found our next new best friend,' he says, taking Cedric by the arm. Stopped in her tracks by the strange pair she has just clapped eyes on, the girl stands alone, the rest of the crowd intent on following the Shamrock.

'What's going on here then ?' says Adam, striding boldly up to the surprised stranger. 'Me and my mate have never seen anything like this before in Sedgefield.'

'Come to that, I've never seen anything like you in Sedgefield.' More intrigued than scared, the girl goes on, pointing towards the mobile in Adam's hand. 'And what were you doing with that contraption ? Some sort of trickery is it ?'

'In a way,' says Cedric, before Adam explains the wild and wonderful tricks of his marvellous magic mobile. The girl listens in silent amazement until he finishes, finally saying, 'I'm Adam, this is Cedric and we're very 'pleased to meet you.'

'And you're very lucky,' adds Cedric, 'because you're the one that can see and hear us this time around. A lass of twelve summers. May we know your name ?'

'I'm Ruby, a jewel of a girl, my gran says. We live with her, me and our Dulcie, that's my little sister, down the bottom there, just past the Golden Lion.' She points to a straggly queue of kids lined up outside the pub waiting for the Shamrock. 'That's where Paddy keeps his hosses and cart,' Ruby tells them. 'In a field out the back. Every year he comes, Easter Saturday and Sunday. Nobody knows his real name, but everybody round here calls him Paddy. Goes with Shamrock.'

They carry on down the street, keeping just enough distance between them and the crowd so Ruby can chatter away without anyone else hearing her.

'Does he came all the way over from Ireland, then ?' Adam asks. 'That's over the sea, Cedric, further away even than Winterton. You can catch a plane in my day, but ...'

Cedric looks puzzled as yet another new word pops so easily from Adam's mouth. 'Like a big bird,' Adam tries to explain, 'you sit inside and it takes you wherever you want to go.'

'Like the magic mobile ?' Cedric smiles.

'I suppose, so, aye, but not so fast.' Adam laughs, as Ruby adds a bit more information to puzzle Cedric.

'We had aeroplanes for fighting in the war, but I've never seen one. I was only four year old when it started, but gran let me go to church when they put the memorial up, cos I was eleven by then. ' Ruby glances down the road. The two big horses slowly turn so that they and the cart are facing up the street, looking towards the church. They calmly take up their position next to the stand pipe in the middle of the road where the ride begins.

'I don't think Paddy's really from Ireland.' Ruby carries on. 'More like a pit yacker. It's a wonder he lets us kids anywhere near his beloved boat. He doesn't seem to like us much. Never cracks his face. Still, I suppose he has to make a living.'

Cedric listens carefully as Ruby prattles on, but Adam's thoughts are on something else.

'Let me get this right, Ruby. The Great War began in 1914, when you were four ...'

Ruby nods, keeping an eye on the growing Shamrock queue, as Adam goes on.

'... and you're 12 now ...'

'Same as us,' adds Cedric, before Adam finishes with a flourish of his hand. 'That means we've landed in 1922 !'

'That's right,' says Ruby, 'Just in time to catch the Easter Sunday Shamrock.' Off she sets running down the street to join the queue, the boys racing after her. 'Stick with me, I'll get you on. Mind, it gets packed out, and we can't leave any gaps, so unless you want somebody sitting on your knee, you'll have to stand.'

'That's OK, we'll get a good view,' grins Adam. 'You'll be able to take some photos,' Cedric adds, quite at home now with the tricks of the magic mobile.

'Ruby ! Ruby !' As they arrive at the tap, starting point for the Shamrock, a shrill little voice cuts through the hubbub of the crowd. Her pigtails streaming out behind her in the breeze, a little girl, no more than five years old runs along the street towards them.

'You have to take me on the Shamrock, our Ruby, Gran says I'm big enough now, but you have to look after me and not let me fall off.'   Out of breath after running down from their little cottage in East Parade and delivering her message at breakneck speed, she stands panting for breath. Holding out her clutched hand and gazing up at her big sister, she adds triumphantly, 'I've got the two pennies – one each !'

Opening her hand, she proudly displays two huge copper coins, their shine dulled by years of use  into a dirty brown. Snatching her fingers closed again over the precious money, the little girl slides her other hand into her sister's. Both girls turn as they hear the Shamrock man call out above the excited clamour of kids eager to get on board.

'Now, just take your time, pack in pushin' and shovin', everybody'll get a go.'

Some of the bigger kids have started jostling about, elbowing their way forward.

'Right, you lot, get t'the back.'

Stretching out his hand towards the motley assortment of kids squashed together in the queue, Paddy points his bony index finger, yellow with nicotine, at the lads.

'Aw, howay mister that's not fair, we've been waitin'

ages.' Grizzling and grumbling, hands stuffed in their pockets, the gang shuffle to the back of the queue.

'I'm not bothered anyway,' says one, shrugging his shoulders. 'I'd rather race the donkeys down East End.'

'Ay, well you'll have to wait on,' Paddy barks back at him. 'There's more than you to think about. Any road, I haven't got the donkeys out the field yet.'

Helping children on with one hand and taking pennies with the other, Paddy starts filling the Shamrock for its tour of the village.

'Up you gan. Fill in from the front now, I want no gaps leavin'.'

Already on board, two little girls, identically dressed down to the red ribbons in their hair, smile smugly down from their seats, up front next to the driver. Jealous but defiant, Dulcie sticks her tongue out at them.

'Them Nuttley twinnies always get the best seats. Wish we could sit up there, Ruby.'

'Aye. Well, you know we cannut,' her big sister replies. 'Costs tuppence each up there and we never have tuppence. Lucky to have a penny.'

Grabbing her sister by the hand, Ruby pushes her two new friends in front of her. Side by side, the lads stand silently in the queue, waiting their chance to sneak on to the Shamrock. 'Come on, our Dulcie, this'll do fine, we'll sit here.' Ruby plonks herself down about half way along the hard wooden plank provided to sit on, shuffling up to let her little sister in beside her. The two lads, invisible to everyone but Ruby, take up their places standing in the middle of the boat.

Giving a quick thumbs up to Ruby, they look out over the side of the Shamrock. To the left, there's the Co-op, all its bottles and jars and tins piled up in pyramids, CWS soap and face powder, white loaves and custard creams. Click goes Adam's camera, then nudging Cedric, he points to Johnny Mowbray's Warehouse round the corner, everything a penny. Pins and needles, sweets, biscuits, treacle, paraffin, Brooke Bond tea, sweet cachous and a penny twist of salt.

'Room for a couple more,' shouts Paddy and a pair of scruffy lads, their knees tanned and scratched from playing out in all weathers, climb on board. Adam and Cedric breathe in to let them past as the new arrivals scramble in to the last two seats.

'Mmm, Calvert's coffee!' To the right of the

Shamrock, the brass shop bell jingles as the door closes behind a new customer, the smell of freshly ground coffee wafting out in to the street. 'Can you smell it, our Dulcie ?' Ruby nods towards the little grocer's shop, as Adam clicks again.

'Waaalk on !' Paddy gently flicks the reins and off they set, shouting and waving to everybody left behind to wait for the next trip. Adam and Cedric grab each other as the cart lurches forward. Ruby catches her breath, but the lads soon steady themselves against the wooden back of the driver's seat. Leaning back, they have a bird's eye view of the village as the heavy horses slowly clop clop up Front Street. Past the smithy on the corner, the forge fire glowing red.

'How do, Paddy,' Mr. Iceton shouts over his stable door. 'Canny day for it.'

'All reet for some, tha' knaas. I never mek a penny oot a' this carry on, mind, Anty. Only do it to give the bairns a bit treat.' Paddy tugs on the skinny little cigarette dangling from the corner of his mouth.

'Give over, man, ya must be rollin' in it. Never mind pleadin' poverty, I bet ye've got a few bob stashed away somewhere.' The blacksmith laughs, but Paddy's face never flickers.

'Ay, and me Rolls Royce is parked round the corner.'

Never breaking stride, the horses walk on, heading towards the top of Front Street, past a few run-down little houses, then Butcher Davison's on the left.

'Look, Dulcie,' Ruby crows, 'your favourite shop, all those lovely sides of meat - beef and lamb and mutton and pork. All that lovely red blood.'

With a nod to Cedric, Adam whispers, ' Remember Joanie and the broth ?' Click, click goes his camera, as Dulcie yells at her sister.

'Behave ! You know I don't like it. I'll tell me gran when we get home. Serve yourself right if I'm sick all over you !'

'Give over you two,' Paddy turns round, looking over his shoulder. 'You'll frighten the hosses. Now, settle down or I'll put yer off.'

The girls meekly do as they're told. They don't want to miss out on their Easter treat. Adam carries on clicking as they pass the church and Cooper's Almshouses. Cedric nods silently at Adam, recognising local landmarks now, just as easily as his modern mate.

'Hello, my dears,' Old Mrs Todd sitting in her doorway waves as they pass.

''Ow do, Hannah,' shouts Paddy, 'I'll be back later for some of them famous cakes of yours.'

'You'll be very welcome, Paddy,' she smiles. 'Mind, don't tell them at the shop will you ? New folks, just in, Crowdens. They've took over from Craggses, selling tea, coffee, all sorts. Cakes, an all.'

'I bet they're not as good as yours, though Hannah,' Paddy gives one of his rare smiles. 'Just like me mother used to bake.'

The Crowdens are all standing outside their shop, on Cross Hill, watching the Shamrock pass by. They've got their own horse and cart, milk churns sitting on the back. The Shamrock's nearly at the top of Front Street now. Brothers Matthew and Ernie, both safely back from the war, wave from the doorway of their shop. Bayston's grocers and provisions, the windows full of jars and bottles, Cadbury's chocolate advertised, half the letters missing. A pure white horse stands quietly outside, ready to take orders round the village in the big delivery cart. She doesn't even look up as the Shamrock clatters past, her bridle clinking in the breeze. Click, click goes the magic mobile. Adam grins at the chance to catch so much history as they pass, Cedric open-mouthed at the sight of such wonders.

As the Shamrock moves slowly on, the girls gaze longingly in to the next shop window - T. Fletcher Draper. Inside, everything is neatly stored away in little wooden drawers with fancy cut glass knobs and white enamel labels – stockings, shirt collars, pillowcases, chair covers. Adam is in his element clicking away at the window, full of Easter bonnets. Leaning over the side to point, Dulcie has to be grabbed back by her big sister.

'Aren't they lovely, Ruby ? I've picked out the one I want. That bonny yellow straw one with pale pink ribbon round and pretend roses on the brim.'

'Don't be daft,' sneers Ruby, 'Can you not see the price tags ? The cheapest costs 1/6. Trust you to pick the dearest - 1/11 that one, near enough a florin.' Sorry to have been so sharp, she adds, smiling, 'Still, as gran says, it costs nowt to look.'

'Whoaaah, there, all reet, roond ye gan,' Paddy gently guides his team round the Black Lion corner past Mona Burdon's, full of sweets the girls can't afford. Peanut brittle, wine gums, liquorice allsorts, macaroons, chewy caramels, jelly babies, coconut ice, Pontefract cakes. 'My belly's rumbling again,' whispers Cedric, longing to taste the sweet treats lined up in huge glass jars in the window.

As the Shamrock passes the Hardwick Arms on the left, Adam snaps another few pictures. 'Hardly changed by my day,' he whispers to Cedric. 'Same as the Manor House back there.' He points back towards the elegant three storey building, the brick wall in front topped with stone pineapples, a sign of welcome and hospitality. 'Offices in there now,' he tells Cedric. 'Manor House 1707.'

Swinging back to look out to the front of the cart, Adam spots a whitewashed cottage on the right, bearing the name White House Farm. Click.

'I'll have to show me Gran this,' he beams. 'She lives along there now – they built houses here in the 1960s. Must have knocked the farmhouse down.'

'Typical,' whispers Cedric, with a grin.

The Shamrock ambles on, passing houses on both sides of the road, another blacksmiths on the left. 'Hello, Mr Alderson !' All the children call across the road, rewarded with a cheery wave. 'That's North End Garage now,' Adam whispers to Cedric, 'They sell petrol and diesel for cars. A bit quicker than the old Shamrock,' he smiles, catching another picture for his memory bank. And another, of the fancy wrought iron gates to Hardwick Park.

'Better get a picture. Not there in my day.' Both lads grab the back of the driver's seat, as Paddy starts to turn the Shamrock round to the right.

Slowly plodding around in a half circle, the two horses gently bring the cart back in to line, ready to trot on down The Lane, back to where they started from. A five bar gate, grubby and moss-covered, provides a perch for some of the lads Paddy had chased earlier on.

'Hurry up, mister, we want a go,' one of them yells across. 'How much longer ?'

'You can't rush these old girls,' Paddy says, giving a gentle flick of his reins. 'We'll be back down the bottom in our own good time. Mebbe ten minutes or so.'

Swinging their legs over to the other side, they leap down from the gate. Then one mad dash down The Lane towards the Golden Lion, whooping and shouting all the way.

'Form a queue at the tap, mind,' Paddy shouts after them, 'and all be ready with your penny.'

# ABOUT TURN !

'Left right, left right, eyes ... left !'

Just vacated by the motley gang of lads waiting their turn on the Shamrock, the five bar gate has a new occupant. One solitary boy, his knees grazed and hair ruffled, sits on top. The toes of his scuffed shoes tucked in to the third bar across. Rolled up cotton shirt sleeves show strong arms tanned by countless days playing out in the fields. A pair of his father's braces struggle to hold up his short trousers, the brown corduroy made smooth by the constant rubbing of grubby hands.

He jumps down off the gate, snapping to attention as the steady tramp tramp of heavy black boots signals the arrival of a couple of soldiers. In khaki battledress, their boots polished and gleaming, caps perched on one side, the two men fall in with the lad's game.

'Reporting for duty, sah !' one of them barks, as both pairs of boots clatter smartly to a halt. Two right arms fly up in salute. Elbows sharp, fingers stiff and straight as knives, eyes staring ahead. The young lad returns their salute, then SNAP ! Arms by their sides and big grins on their faces. At ease now, one tall, the other a bit shorter, they stop for a word.

'You're getting better at this, son,' says the taller one. 'We'll have you square bashing yet.'  Looking round to check nobody else has seen their little game, neither soldier spots two other lads, tucked away out of sight. Bobbed down behind a scruffy bit of hedge running away from the farm gate, Cedric and Adam watch and listen, holding their breath. The men don't linger though. Rubbing his hands together and giving them a final clap, the smaller soldier says,  'Better be off then, son. Nice to see you again and all that, but the sarge has sent us up the village to get the post and if we're not back pronto, he'll have us on a fizzer. TTFN !'

'Tata for now!' the lad replies, giving a final salute as the two soldiers head off to the village.

'Excuse me.' Adam slowly sticks his head out from behind the hedge, Cedric peeking past his shoulder. 'Can we have a word ?'

The other lad jumps back in surprise.  Instantly covering up his shock at being observed, he drops his saluting arm to his side and strolls towards them. 'See that, having a word with the lads from the camp. They all know me, come up here every day. Never seen you two afore.' Scrambling out from their hiding place behind the hedge, Adam and Cedric introduce themselves. 'Pleased to meet you I'm sure, Sam's the name, Sam Brown, like the army belt, you know, only that has an -e on the end I think. Of Browne, I mean. Any road, most folks call us Sammy.'

Pleased to have landed at the feet of such a chatty new friend, Adam tells Sammy about their travels with the magic mobile. Stunned into silence by its peculiar powers, Sammy listens spellbound, his mouth and eyes growing wider with each new trick. Finally, Adam explains how they come to be talking to him, here and now.

'So,' he says, 'one minute we're standing up as Paddy turns the cart down The Lane, the next Bingo ! Dropped like stones as the Shamrock vanishes. We nipped over that stile and hid behind the hedge when we heard the soldiers' boots. You didn't see us. Too busy saluting.'

Checking around for places he knows, Cedric spots the iron gates opposite, the pond nearby. Smoke snakes up from the chimney of a big red brick house set in a large garden. 'I've not seen that afore,' he says. 'Has time moved on again ?'

'Connor Lodge,' says Adam. 'Has a big wall round it in my day. Used to be the doctor's before we got the new one down the village.'

'Still is,' says Sammy. 'Been there as long as I remember. They had to put that bit porch on the front for the blackout.'

Seeing the puzzled look on both faces, Sammy explains that everyone in the village has to put up thick black curtains so that no lights show in the darkness.

'There's a war on, you know,' says Sammy, in the same tone of voice he's heard so often from adults around the village. 'Twice as many people in Sedgefield now the soldiers are here. Come from all over the country, they do, Northern Ireland an 'all. The Royal Ulster Rifles. They're in the other camp down at the racecourse, yon side of the village.' He waves his left arm to a point away in the distance. Turning to the right, he goes on, 'And there's the army hospital up the road. They brought lads there from Dunkirk. 1940. On the run from Jerry, you know.'

Swinging back round, he looks fondly towards his

favourite camp.

'This is the best one, though. Built special to keep an eye out for enemy aircraft. Searchlight Battalion it's called. Ack Ack guns an' all that.'

'Ack Ack ?' repeats Cedric, frowning. 'Guns ? Search – light ?' Out of his depth with all these new words. 'Tell me what you mean,' he pleads.

'I can do better than that, lad,' says Sammy, 'if you and your pal can help me out with this here mobile doodah.' Adam now looks just as puzzled as his Saxon friend. Sammy goes on.

'You reckon it makes you invisible, so I can see and hear you, but nobody else can ?'

'That's right,' says Cedric, 'because you're twelve, same as us and you spotted us first.'

'That'll come in handy,' says Sammy. 'You could have a wander round the camp and nobody'd see you. I've always wanted a proper look in. Do you think you can make me invisible an'all ?'

'Dunno,' Adam shrugs, laughing at this novel idea. 'Never tried, nobody's asked before.' He and Cedric look at each other and straight back at Sammy, staring hopefully at them now.

After a brief moment to consider, Cedric grins. 'As you always say, Adam, worth a try.'

Excited at the prospect of taking photos inside the army camp to add to his growing collection, Adam is worried that they could lose this new friend before the fun even begins.

'What if I click the wrong button ?' he says. 'We could end up anywhere, well, anytime. We've never left Sedgefield so far.'

'Tell you what, I'll do you a deal.'  Ferreting around in his pocket, Sammy fishes out all sorts of booty. None of it worth a penny, but priceless to him. Bits of string, a couple of stripy mints covered in fluff, a tiny green crab apple, a rubber band, a forked twig. 'Gonna make a catapult, when I get a minute,' he says, carefully placing the last two items on top of the farm gate. 'Great for catching squirrels. You get a penny each for their tails you know, if you take them in to the police station.'

Adam pulls a face at the idea of doing the deed, just for a measly penny. Rummaging in his other pocket, Sammy goes on, 'Oh aye, classed as vermin, like rats, they are. All the kids are after them. My mate Tosher's caught loads.'

Still puzzled as to what this deal might be, the lads watch fascinated as Sammy drags yet more plunder from his pocket. A couple of glass marbles, one lead soldier, a dog-eared cardboard bus ticket, a big copper penny, a stub of pencil. Finally, a filthy old hanky folded corner to corner and tied in a knot. Holding it carefully in the palm of his grubby hand, Sammy opens it up to reveal the treasure inside. A mangled bit of metal, dark grey, no shine to it, a rainbow of colours streaking across the top.

'If you make us invisible, Adam,' he says, gulping at the prospect of parting with this hard-won jewel, 'I'll give you me bit of shrapnel.'

'What is it ?' asks Cedric, reaching out a finger to touch the crinkled metal, lying like a twisted stone in Sammy's hand.

'Wor is it ? Wor is it ?' Sammy cries in disbelief. 'Only the best bit of shrapnel in my whole collection, that's what. Came from the big raid the other night.'

Enjoying his new position as war expert, Sammy holds his captive audience spellbound as he takes them through the events of that night. They fall silent as he begins, quietly at first, building the tension, looking from one boy to the other as he unrolls his gripping tale.

'About 8 o'clock, the sirens went. The sky was lit up like daylight. Over at the Kennels, beside Hardwick Park, our searchlight had Jerry in its beam.' He sweeps a raised hand through the air, his head tipped towards the imagined glow in the sky. Cedric listens intently, gripped, if a little lost in this wartime world. Sammy explains. 'That's like a big torch, Cedric, that you can turn round and point where you like.'

'Thank you, Sammy,' Cedric smiles, glad of the help. 'And Jerry ?'

'The Germans, of course, the enemy, the ones we've been fighting the last three years. Any road, back at the camp, our lads are rattling away on the Bofors guns.'

'Anti-aircraft, right ?' asks Adam, trying to keep up with the break-neck speed of Sam's story telling. They'd done the second world war at school, so he knew a bit about it, but nothing like this eye-witness account from their new friend.

'Yeah, ack-ack, that's right, mate,' Sammy nods, eager to get on with the rest of his thrilling story. 'That's where the shrapnel comes from, the shells when they hit the ground. You should see the sparks fly !' All three lads are grinning now, caught up in the excitement.

'Then there was this whistling sound and WHAM !' he shouts, then stops a moment for effect. 'A load of bombs dropped. Landed in the fields over Butterwick way. Right in line with the camp, though. That's what they were after, I reckon. The draught whooshed right through the village, people were blew off their feet. Some got black faces from soot coming down the chimneys. It was great !' He finishes with a wide grin, out of breath, but full of pride in having told his tale so well.

'And you found the shrapnel that night ?' Cedric stands in awe of this new hero.

'No fear,' says Sammy. 'I was down the village shelter with me Mam while all that was going off. Had to get up early the next day. All the lads were out at the crack of dawn to get the best bits, but I think I did all right.' Cedric can hardly believe his eyes when Sammy hands him the precious lump of shrapnel. 'Here you are, son, you can have a hold for a bit if you like.'

Cupping both hands together to make a safe place for the hard-won trophy, Cedric gazes down at the ugly chunk of twisted metal, so important to Sammy.

'And you'd give us this if we can make you invisible ?' he asks, his voice faint with respect.

'I'd give anything for a wander round that camp,' says Sammy, longingly. 'They've got all sorts in there you know, even their own hospital and dentist.'

'That's for looking after you when you're ill, Cedric,' explains Adam. 'Or if you've got a bad tooth. It's all on the National Health now, you know, Sammy. Free like.'

Cedric has never had medical help, free or not, except for the herbs his mother gathers to make potions. Still, he'd like to see inside the camp, if only so that he can keep the shrapnel so kindly promised. With a scowl and shaking his head, Sammy goes on.

'But you'd never get past that sentry box. There's always someone on guard duty, night and day. But if I was invisible, now ... '

'You could sneak in with us.' Cedric finishes for him. 'And tell us what's what,' adds Adam.

All three lads are as keen as mustard now, dead set on

getting into the army camp and having a good look round, under the magic mobile's cloak of invisibility. But how to get Sammy in with them ? That's the question. As they stand puzzling over the problem, the tramp of boots breaks through their thoughts. The two soldiers back from post office duty.

'Now then, Sammy,' the taller one says, 'You still here ? Must be past your dinner time.'

Laughing, his mate adds, 'Ain't you got no mates to play with ? You should be kicking a ball about somewhere, a nice day like this. Not hanging about on your own.'

Sammy nods and grins, pleased that the soldiers can't see the other two lads leaning against the farm gate. 'I'm all right,' he says, 'might nip home for some nosh just now. I'll be gone  in a jif.' The soldiers wave as they walk smartly on towards the camp gate.

'See you then, son.'

'I hope not,' mumbles Sammy, turning back towards the lads. 'Not if you two can make us  disappear.'

Grinning broadly, Adam says, 'We've been having a think while you were chatting to your soldier pals. Now, we haven't tried this before, but it always works for Doctor Who.'

'On the telly,' adds Cedric, helpfully.

'On the what?' Sammy's turn to be puzzled.

'Like the radio... erm.... wireless, only with pictures.' Adam tries to help out.

'Pictures ? You mean, the cinema, like the Savoy down the village ?' Sammy asks.

'Like that, yeah, only smaller, and in your house. Everybody has them in my day. Flat screen, HD, Sky. I have my own in my bedroom.' Adam rattles on. 'No cinema, though. Savoy, was it ? That's gone. Massive multi screens in the big towns though.'

Sammy and Cedric look at each other, shaking their heads. Both bewildered by Adam's world. Trying to come back to the point, Adam says, 'Anyway, never mind that, the thing is, we've come up with a way to get you invisible.'

Carefully putting the shrapnel into the pouch on his belt, Cedric takes over. Reaching out he grasps Adam and Sammy by a hand each.

'It's simple, we form a circle, like this. Come on, join up.' The three lads stand, looking at each other, their hands linked.

'Now what ?' asks Sammy. 'I don't feel any different. Can you still see us ?

'Well, yeah,' says Adam, 'but that proves nowt. You can see us two and nobody else can.'

'True,' says Sammy. 'Should we say a magic word or something ?'

'Like 'please', you mean ?' Adam laughs. 'That's the magic word in our house.'

'Mine an'all,' Sammy agrees. 'Me mother's always saying it. "What's the magic word, our Samuel?" Gets on your wick.'

The two lads have a good laugh, but Cedric quietly lets go of their hands. His face very serious, he says, 'The only magic we need is in your pocket, Adam.'

The others calm down again, taking Cedric's wise words to heart.

'You're right, Ced,' says Adam, ' but what numbers do we push to make Sammy vanish ?'

'And how will we know when I've gone ?' adds Sammy, worried he might get caught wandering round the camp.

'That's easy.' Cedric is well in command now. 'You say the men are used to seeing you at the gate, near the ... erm ... box ?'

'The sentry box, aye,' smiles Sammy. 'I'm there every day, like the bad penny they say. They never chase us, but. Always say "How do?" and that.'

'So, if you go over and they don't speak ...' Cedric goes on, but Sammy finishes for him.

'... I'll know they cannut see us !' Beaming all over his face, Sammy sticks out his hands for the other lads to clasp. 'Howay, then, let's get on with it.'

Adam holds back for a moment, his mobile clutched in his left hand. 'Hang on a sec. I'll need to key some numbers in first. What shall we try this time, fellas ?'

'Why not this year, the one we're in now ?' Cedric suggests.

'Good as any, Cedric. OK, Sammy, fire away,' says Adam, his fingers poised over the keys. He taps in the numbers as Sammy slowly spells out '1 – 9 – 4 – 2'.

Quickly slipping the phone back into his pocket, Adam grabs Sammy's hand. Reaching arms out on both sides, Cedric closes the circle. Adam whispers, 'And maybe a bit of help from the magic word.'

All three lads grasp hands, close their eyes tight and yell in unison, 'PLEE-EE-ASE !'

# INSIDE HARDWICK CAMP

The large wooden gate leading in to the army camp stands open, as usual. To the left, two soldiers, not those Sammy had spoken to earlier, stand on duty. One bolt upright inside the sentry box, his rifle by his side, ready for action. The other at ease, hands behind his back, his feet apart. Behind them a low stone wall, whitewashed. A couple of silver milk churns await the farmer's collection.

The three lads stand stock still for a moment. In line, Sammy in the centre, grasping the hands of Adam and Cedric on either side. All silent. They face the soldiers. Five pairs of eyes stare straight ahead.

'Now then,' Sammy mutters, smiling nervously at the soldiers. 'All right, lads ?'

Not a word in reply. Either side of him, the other two lads try a silly salute. Nothing in return.

'I think we've cracked it,' Adam whispers, looking sidelong at Sammy but keeping his eyes front. 'You say they always talk to you, even on duty ?'

'Yeah,' says Sammy, grinning in disbelief. 'Just to say hello and that, they never ignore us.'

'Well, they're ignoring you now, my friend,' says Cedric, calmly. 'Shall we walk on ?'

Firmly clasping hands, the three lads turn towards the entrance, their faces creased with joy. 'I can't believe it worked,' says Sammy, 'that mobile thing of yours is dead clever. You should give it to the army. We'd have Hitler licked in no time.'

'A very nasty man who started off this war, Cedric,' Adam explains. 'Little fella with a stiff arm and a daft 'tache.'

'Like Charlie Chaplin,' adds Sammy, with a grin. 'In the fillums. Only he's a real laugh.' Sticking his feet out in a V shape, he waddles along, the lads either side holding on to him.

'I'll do the stick, Sammy,' says Adam, 'You haven't a hand free. You too, Cedric, like this.'

Clinging to Sammy in the middle, the others join in, twirling invisible walking sticks, one either side. They take a few waddling steps along the path leading away from the gate. Soon, all three are stopped in their tracks as they take in the view of the army camp laid out in front of them. A huge central square. Around it, six identical wooden huts with sloping tin roofs.

'Oh, great,' says Adam, 'I'll be able to get some brill photos. That's another of my mobile's magic tricks, Sammy. Only need one hand, so I can still keep you under cover.' He fumbles in his pocket for the phone and starts clicking away as the guided tour begins.

'They'll be the spiders,' says Sammy keeping his voice low, even though he knows only Cedric and Adam can hear him. 'That's what the soldiers call them huts, spiders. They say when it rains you'd think the sky was falling in, it's that noisy.'

Noise seems to be the order of the day as dozens of pairs of army boots clatter around the camp. Crowds of soldiers, khaki-clad from top to toe. Thick trousers, too warm on this summer day, battle dress tunics curved in at the waist, buttons Brassoed till they gleam. Fresh faced and eager, some look little older than Sammy and his mates. Short cropped hair, glossy with Brylcreem. Forage caps tilted to one side, lower over the right eye. Flattened into a sharp crease then knocked apart with the edge of the hand. At the front, one above the other, two little brass buttons shiny with elbow grease. Alongside, the circular cap badge of the Northumberland Fusiliers. In the golden centre, Saint George slays the dragon.

'What you doing, soldier ?' A gruff voice rings out across the parade ground. A raw recruit, his foot barely touching the grey tarmac of the square, jumps back as if he's been shot. Arms rammed down by his sides, neck stiff and eyes round with fear, he looks straight ahead.

'Ow many times 'ave I told you ?' bellows the sergeant. 'No short cuts !'

'Yes sarge, no sarge, sorry sarge,' the young soldier mumbles. 'Just nipping to the billet for my pay book.'

'Just nipping to the billet for my pay book - sarge!' The last word rings out loud and clear. His chin snaps out and in again, his neck stiff. Clenched into a fist, his left hand sits behind his back. The fingers of his right hand curl around a fine wooden swagger stick, tucked up and under his right arm.

'I don't care if you're dashing to the bedside of your dying grandmother. You – go - round – the - path !' barks the older man, sharply pointing out all four sides of the path with his stick.  'That there square is sacred. What is it, soldier ?'

'Sacred sarge, sorry sarge,' mutters the young squaddie, standing stiffly to attention even though he's shaking in his boots. 'And don't you forget it, lad.' The sergeant's voice drops to a low murmur before a final blast, 'Get on with it then !'

The terrified soldier scuttles off, his boots clattering along the path and down the steps to his billet. With a smug smile and ramrod straight back, the sergeant major marches on. Every clump of his shiny black boots echoes across the camp. Only once he steps into a distant hut dare the boys breathe.

'Cor, I wouldn't like to cross him,' whispers Sammy. 'I bet he takes no prisoners.'

'I'm glad he can't see us,' says Cedric softly, clinging harder than ever to Sammy's hand.

'Is that the parade ground, do you think, Sam ?' Adam asks, just as quietly.

'Aye, where they do the marching and that. Square bashing they call it. I can't believe I'm looking at it.' Struck dumb for only a moment, the old Sammy soon returns, full of cheek and confidence.  Dragging the other two lads along either side of him, he points out the sergeants' quarters.

'Where old Thunder Guts went in. Next door that'll be the officers' mess, for the top brass. A bit posher than the lads' billets I bet. Mind, I've heard there's hot baths and showers for the ordinary soldiers. Better than what we have at home. A tin bath once a week.'

'Whether you need it or not !' Adam and Sammy chorus, laughing. Cedric has, of course, never heard of a bath, tin or otherwise, and a shower might be a drop of rain on the field. But, right now, he's busy gazing up at a large sign hanging above the next hut.

'What's those marks up there, Sammy?' he asks, pointing up at the letters N – A – A – F - I.

'Summat to do with Army, Navy and Air Force, but some of the lads say it means Never 'Ave Any Fags In.' Sammy grins. 'Sort of a shop, see. The lads'll give us a bar of chocolate when they have it in. Canteen, as well. You can get a cup of char and a wad.'

'Speak English, will you,' Adam smiles. 'You lost Cedric back at the fags. And you'd better explain  char and a wad.'

'Cup of tea, of course and a sarnie, sandwich, Spam usually. You get a lot of that these days, Cedric.  Pink meat, comes in a tin. Put it between two slices of bread. I love it, but you can get a bit sick of it.'

Not stopping to explain what a tin is or how you get meat inside it, the lads carry on walking, their hands firmly clasped together. 'And fags ?' asks Cedric. The other boys look at each other, stuck as to how to explain cigarettes to their Saxon mate.

'Smokes, tabs, cigs,' says Sammy, as if giving Cedric a host of other names will help him understand.

'To put it simply, mate,' Adam explains gently, 'it's a round stick made of paper filled with this dried leaf called tobacco. You stick it in your mouth and set fire to it.'

'Why ?' asks Cedric, once again puzzled by the strange habits of these modern people.

'Search me,' says Adam, 'Filthy habit, my Mam says. Most places have banned it now.'

'Have they ?' Sammy looks shocked. 'Everybody smokes round here. Even me, if I can I nick one of me grandad's Woodbines. Mind, now they're on the ration, he has them counted in the packet.'

Keeping to the path, the stern words of the RSM still ringing in their ears, they soon reach the NAAFI hut. Even though they can't be seen, the lads hang back, none of them daring to push the door open.

'Pity,' says Sammy, 'There's a billiard table in there, we could have had a game.'

'Might look a bit funny, balls flying around the table with nobody there,' Adam points out.

'Oh yeah, never thought of that,' Sammy laughs, just as they spot a brightly coloured poster.

'Thursday – 18.00 hours – Dancing to the Fernley Mitchell Band — free entrance.'

'They have a lot of dances,' Sammy tells them, 'the lasses come down from the village. You should see them, all dolled up. Legs painted with gravy browning, beetroot for lipstick and their hair rolled up like a sausage.' Sucking in his cheeks, Sammy totters along on tiptoe.  Arms linked to stay invisible, the other lads mimic him. A giggling trio of village girls out for a night of fun. After a few high-heeled steps, the boys drop back down on to flat feet and grab hands again. All laughing stops, as three real girls walk towards them. In uniform just like the men, except for a skirt instead of trousers, flat black shoes and a soft cap with a peak. Chatting as they walk, the girls don't see three dozy lads standing back to let them pass.

'ATS,' whispers Sammy. 'Girl soldiers. I bet they're off to The Ops Room. With all the maps and that. Like in that film I saw down the Savoy - 'Target for Tonight', I think it was. They have to be dead good, so the searchlights point the right way when Jerry comes over. They don't just answer the phone and drive jeeps, you know.'

Still holding hands, the lads carry on to the far side of the parade ground. 'Cor, look at that,' gasps Sammy. Propped up on three legs of black metal, a long tube, the same dull colour, points towards the sky. Piled up on all sides, sacks filled with sand steady the metal feet. 'The Lewis gun.' Sammy gazes in awe at the machine gun he's heard so much about. Guarded as it is by two soldiers, the lads can't get too close, despite being invisible.

Keeping a little distance away, and still hanging on to his two mates, Sammy nods towards a flattened circle at one end of the gun. 'The ammo goes in there, see, in that big drum.' Pulling the other lads with him, Sammy crouches down on one knee. The two soldiers on guard duty have no idea there are three young spies in the camp. Sammy drags the lads closer to the gun.  Pretending to look through the viewfinder on top of the gun barrel, he scrunches one eye shut. Reaching both hands forward as if holding the gun, he swings from side to side. Two other hands shoot forward at the same time and the other lads swing with him.

The two duty soldiers don't hear a thing as he rattles out the machine gun noise, 'Eeh – eeh -- eeh – eeh --- eeeh !'

'Did you get them, Sam ?' Adam smiles, as they all struggle back to their feet, still holding hands. 'Not this time, two Heinkels and a Focke. Got clean away.' Looking from one to the other of his two new friends, Sammy steps away from the gun. 'Thanks, fellas,' he says cheekily to the soldiers.  'Keep your eyes peeled, mind. Jerry could be over any minute.'

 Relishing his role as war expert and official guide, he leads his two mates along the tarmac path at the top edge of the parade ground. 'Better get on, lads,' he says. 'Still plenty to see.' They stroll along together, hand in hand, taking in the sights around them. The parade ground and path are set up high, the huts around them on all four sides lower down. To the right, they can see for miles across open countryside. Cedric stops, so the others do too.

'I hear sheep,' he says, looking into the distance. 'That must be my father's feld yonder.'

'Cedric's father, Cedd, owns all the land over there,' Adam tells Sammy, pointing with his mobile, clicking a photo at the same time. 'Hence the name, Cedd's Feld, Sedgefield.'

'Gerraway !' says Sammy. 'I thought it was cos it's all boggy, you know, sedge.'

'That is true also.' Cedric peers across the landscape, a little worried about the sheep he had forgotten until now. 'I have to be wary of that when I tend the flock. I hope they are safe.'

'They'll be safer back in your day than beasts are now, with bombs dropping all over,' says Sammy, suddenly very serious. 'And no fellas to look after them,' cos they're away fighting.'

Solemn faced, all three boys gaze across at the peaceful scene beyond the camp.

'Hard to believe there's a war on, isn't it ?' Sammy's brave smile cheers them all up.

Turning back towards the camp, he leads them further along the path. Pointing to a hut much taller than the rest, he says. 'That'll be one of the garages, I bet. They have quite a few for the Motor Transport. That high one'll be for when they're mending the searchlights. There's loads of ' em, you know , all along the coast, right to Blackhall.'

As they stop to take a closer look, the garage door opens. A couple of soldiers step out for a breather. Tunics off, shirt sleeves rolled up, elastic braces buttoned into thick khaki trousers. One mops a mixture of sweat and motor oil from his brow, the other rolls his shoulders to ease his aching muscles. 'Five minutes only,' barks a voice from inside.

'Right, sarge.' Together they shout in reply, then tutting quietly, shake their heads as they move round to the side of the hut for a quick smoke. Smiling at the cheek of the soldiers, the lads, glad to be in on the secret, move further along the path. A group of four ATS girls, chattering as they walk, head towards another hut, ready for work in Motor Transport.

'There's women doing all sorts now,' says Sammy, sounding much older than his twelve years. Helping out on the farms. And wearing trousers ! Land Girls, you know, come from all over. There's a hostel in the village. POWs, they have to help as well. '

'Prisoners of War, Cedric,' Adam explains, as they wander slowly along the path.

'Aye, that's right,' says Sammy. 'There's Germans, they come over from Windlestone Hall. That's a posh house a few miles off. They're not too bad really, but the Eyeties !' He stops for a moment, shaking his head, lost for words to show how he feels.

'Italians ?' asks Adam, more for Cedric's benefit than his own. 'They come from Italy, mate, the same as our Roman friend from the park.' Reminded once again about the place where he'd left his flock, Cedric nods, with a faint smile.

'That's right, Eyeties. Idle beggars, my granddad says. Me and me mates make game of them when we see them in the village. They wear chocolate brown tunics with a massive yellow circle on the back. Like a big bullseye. Great target. Good for hoying goosegogs at.'

'Gooseberries, Ced, 'Adam explains. 'Little round green fruits, dead sour and rock hard. Good for hoying though, eh Sammy ? Or throwing, if you're talking posh, like. '

The three lads walk on, smiling, so used to holding hands they don't even think about it. They head back towards the gate, their tour almost finished. All around, soldiers of all shapes and sizes step smartly around the parade ground. Not one sets a foot on the sacred space. Nothing to stop three daft lads, though. Especially as they can't be seen.

'Howay, lads,' Sammy yells, dragging the others on to the tarmac with him. 'Time for a spot of square bashing. Bags I be sergeant !'

After a bit of giggling and shoving, all three lads, on Sammy's command, stand smartly to attention. Not easy holding hands. Barking out orders like he's born to it, Sammy moves his ragged little troop across the parade ground. 'Eyes front ! Quick March !'

Not quite in step, but not bad for raw recruits.
'Left right left right left right left !'

Arms swinging, still holding hands, Sammy keeps the marching tempo. Adam butts in with some new words. 'Left, left, I had a good job and I left.'

Grinning, they keep tramping forward as Sammy gives the order, 'Eyes right !' All three heads snap to one side. And straight back, as they spot the real sergeant stepping out smartly along the path. 'Eyes front !' Even though he can't see or hear them, the lads are not taking any chances.

'About turn !' yells Sammy, as they hurtle towards the gate. 'Fall out !'

And that's just what they do. Fall out of the gate and on to the road outside the camp. All three in a tumbling, gasping, laughing heap. Not holding hands. Leaping to their feet, they grab at each other, their backs towards the sentry box. Too late.

'Come back here, my lad !' The boys freeze as they hear the sergeant's fearsome roar.

'You two useless lumps, what you think you're doing ? Letting a stranger in the camp !'

The soldiers spring to attention, saluting as he strides across to their duty post.

The lads cling to each other, huddled together in a desperate attempt to stay hidden.

'It's me he's after,' whispers Sammy. 'You two get away. Go on, scarper !' Fixed to the spot, neither lad wants to leave their new good friend.

'So long, Sammy,' whispers Adam, squeezing his hand. Cedric gulps back a tear, murmuring, 'I'll look after your shrapnel.' Sammy nods gently, returning each squeeze with a smile.

 Dropping their hands, he turns slowly to meet the sergeant's furious stare. He peers in to Sammy's face.

'What you up to, laddie ? This is army property,' he bellows, 'not a kiddie's playground.'

Standing tall, arms smartly by his sides like a proper soldier, Sammy holds his head high.

Now safely beyond the gate, outside the camp, side by side Adam and Cedric stand watching. With a final salute to Sammy, Adam calls 'Left turn !' 'Forward march !' cries Cedric.

They turn in unison and step smartly towards the village.

# A VISIT TO ST ED'S

'I hope Sammy is safe,' says Cedric, worried lines crinkling his brow. 'With that angry man.'

'He'll be all right,' replies Adam brightly. 'Just get a telling off, then chased  home. He'll probably catch us up any minute.'

Cedric perks up at the thought of seeing Sammy again. 'I hope so,' he says, as they carry on walking in step towards the village. Before long, they notice some changes. No big red house, for a start. But fields still stretch away to the left. Opposite, the fancy park gates, the slimy pond next to the blacksmiths. Cottages line the road, a handful of little shops. Some they remember from their Shrove Tuesday Ball Game with Johnny.

'Not sure what's going on here, Cedric,' says Adam, looking around for clues. 'Remember the girls at the butchers told us about the air raid shelter on the green ?' He points across towards the spot where it should be. No sign of it. Hardwick Arms, the Manor House, Town

Farm – all present and correct. A few poor looking houses. A few poor looking people to go with them. None take any notice of two lads wandering down High Street.

Beside the church, they spot the square block of the school house, once a prison. 'Remember,' says Adam, 'Johnny told us he'd just left.'

'There's his house,' adds Cedric, pointing across to the little cottage, 'where we had pancakes under the table.'

'I could do with them right now,' says Adam.

'And some of Joan's mother's broth,' adds Cedric, as they walk on towards the almshouses. No butcher's shop alongside, though. Opposite, across the muddy road, a row of simple little houses. No steps, no Savoy cinema.

'Have they knocked it down ?' asks Cedric, touching in his simplicity.

Draping an arm over his mate's shoulder, Adam tells him, 'No, Ced, I'd say they haven't built it yet.' He adds gently, 'I don't think we'll be seeing Sammy again any time soon. Looks like we've slipped time zones again, mate.'

'But we didn't do anything,' says Cedric. Feeling in his belt pouch, he's glad to find the shrapnel safely there, a memento of Sammy and his wartime adventure. 'Have you the mobile still?'

Pulling the phone from his pocket, Adam checks it for damage. 'Looks OK,' he says.

'Maybe it took a knock when  we all fell in that heap outside the camp gates.'

'And sped us on us to another time ?' asks Cedric.

'More likely back to an earlier time,' says Adam. 'I wonder which bit of the past we've dropped into now.'

Walking away from the almshouses, the lads head towards the church. Craning their necks to get a good look at the tower. 'Good old St Ed's,' says Adam, 'doesn't change much.'

As they walk round the corner, he tells Cedric there's been a church in Sedgefield since about 900 AD. A simple wooden one at first. A bit later, when the Normans came over from France in 1066, they built a stone church with rounded arches. After another 200 years or so, a much bigger church sprung up. 'Took ten years to build,' says Adam. 'They finished it in 1256, just in time for the first Ball Game.'

'How do you know all this ?' asks Cedric, impressed at the historic facts his pal has at his fingertips.

'Sunday School,' grins Adam. 'I used to go every week when I was little. The teachers told us bits and bobs all the time. Can't remember all of it.' Grabbing Cedric's arm, he pulls them both to a halt, looking towards the church. 'I know there should be a lych gate here, though.'

No war memorial either. 'That cross should be there from the first world war,' says Adam. 'They added a few more names after Sammy's war finished.'

'We've gone back in time, then ?' asks Cedric.

'Looks like it, mate,' says Adam. 'Question is, how far ?'

As they stroll along the rough path towards the church, Adam tells Cedric a bit more.

'Not many St Edmund's churches about, you know. Archbishop of Canterbury, he was, Edmund Rich. Good name, that, cos they were an'all, rectors of Sedgefield. Very rich. In the old days, that is. Rolling in it. You should see the house they had to live in.'

By now, the lads have reached the church. Set into a stone arch, the heavy wooden door is firmly closed. Adam tries turning the large round handle. Like a twisted rope of copper. He shakes out his right hand, fingers aching with the effort. 'No use, Ced, it won't budge.' Cedric steps forward to have a go. His strong hands, used to dragging sheep from muddy fields, strain to turn the handle. Now it's his turn to give in, blowing cool air on to both hands, shaking from the wrists.

'Locked, mate,' says Adam. 'Same as in my day. Some people nick anything. They even took a brass lady from the wall once. Turned up years later in a pub somewhere.'

The boys stand looking at the locked church door, defeated for the time being. Adam jokes, 'I could do with a sonic screwdriver, like Doctor Who. That would get us in.'

'Another job for the magic mobile, maybe ?' suggests Cedric, hoping for a miracle. Smiling, Adam reaches into his pocket. 'You have great faith in this little beauty, my old mate.' 'Worth a try !' says Cedric, wondering how on earth Adam is going to do the trick this time. After a brief moment's thought, Adam says, 'Tell you what, Ced, let's try texting it this time. That's words, not numbers. Open sesame and all that.' Naturally, Cedric hasn't a clue what he's talking about. 'Aladdin, you know, the panto. Oh, no, you don't do you ?  Well, anyway, his wicked uncle locks him in a cave and he can't get out until he says the magic words.'

'Open sesame ?' asks Cedric. 'Spot on, mate,' says Adam, his thumbs already hovering over the mobile buttons. In no time at all, he has the letters keyed in. Finally tapping SEND, he points the phone towards the huge locked door. With a gentle creak, slowly it swings open. 'Wow !' Clutching his miraculous mobile tightly in his left hand, Adam drapes his right arm over Cedric's shoulder. 'Come on, my son, time for the guided tour.'

As the boys walk in, they see another door, opposite and almost identical to the one they've just come through. 'They used to open it to let the devil out,' explains Adam, going on to tell him about the marble font, just in front of them. 'Where babies are baptised,' he says. 'That's their first entry into the church, see.' Cedric nods slowly, struggling to understand the ways of this modern world.  'So it has to be near the door, the way in. Supposed to be pretty old, that font,' says Adam. '15th century or so.'

Just beyond the font, he points out the stairs leading up to the church tower. 'Where they ring the bells. A bit of a climb, but you get a great view from the top. Been up there, Mediaeval Fayre Day.'

'We saw the rector start the ball game from there,' Cedric remembers. 'That's right, Ced,' says Adam, 'Or he might have sent the young curate up all them steps. Why have a dog and bark yourself, as me granda says.'

The lads turn away from the tower steps and walk together down the central aisle of the church, Cedric entranced by the golden stones of its great arches, carved pillars holding up the stout oak roof.

'Thirteenth century, them, mate,' says Adam, proud of the church although he hasn't been inside since his auntie Nicola's wedding a couple of years earlier.

'What are these openings here, Adam ?' Cedric points up to the great pointed windows, many filled with colourful stained glass images.

'To let the light in, mate,' Adam tells him. 'And keep the birds out perhaps,' adds Cedric.

'Aye, and the rain,' Adam grins. 'A lot of them are in memory of people, rich ones, mostly.'

The boys stop for a moment, sitting on one of the wooden pews near the front of the church. 'A bit hard on your bum,' says Adam. 'Glad they got some comfy chairs eventually. Mind, way back, like in your time, Ced, I expect people had to stand.'

In front of them, a finely carved wooden screen. 'Put there in the 1600's,' says Adam, 'by Bishop Cosin. Very pretty an' all that, but it makes it hard to see what's going on at the altar. Unless you're in the choir, like, but they'd never have let me join. Voice like a bullfrog, me Dad says.' The lads laugh quietly, as they stand to walk through the central arch of the screen, past the ornate choir stalls to the altar. 'Have a look at this, Ced,' says Adam, pointing to a large black slab in the floor to the left of the altar. 'Remember the almshouses ?'

'And Joanie's broth ?' Cedric licks his lips at the memory. 'Well, this is the gravestone of Thomas Cooper, the guy who left the money to build them. Look, it even says how much the old folks were to be given.' Very impressed, even though he can't read a word, Cedric asks, 'Is he down there, then, under that stone ?' Lost for an answer for once in his life, Adam has to admit he doesn't know. 'Shouldn't think so, most of them are outside in the graveyard.'

Without pausing for breath, he sets off at a gallop, back down the main aisle. 'Howay, Ced. It's getting a bit chilly in here. Let's go and see if we can get a look at the rectory.'

Cedric chases after him, catching up with his impetuous friend just as he reaches the main door. 'Thank you, St. Edmund,' Cedric says quietly, taking a final look back at the beautiful church. Adam grabs his arm, pulling him out into the warmer air of the churchyard. 'Race you down the Vicar's Dash ! ' They run together along a narrow path running away from the church towards a little wrought iron gate. A few steps down lead to another gate opposite, this one made of wood. 'A short cut !' yells Adam. They are just about to cross over when a voice stops them in their tracks. ' Hey, you boys ! What are you up to ?'

A young lad, about their age, dressed in a long black coat, knee breeches and stockings, strides towards them.

'I guess we're not still in the war years, then, Cedric,'

mumbles Adam. 'Up to now, I've only seen a get-up like that on telly.'

'We mean no harm,' says Cedric, trying to keep the peace. Walking towards the new boy, Adam smiles. 'Just showing my mate here the church.'

'Only my father is allowed to use this path.' The boy in black scowls, holding his head stiffly

'Sounds like you when we first met, Ced.' After all the adventures they've been through, Adam is not to be put off by a snooty attitude in a frock coat. 'You didn't like me stepping on your father's land either.'

'My father is a shepherd,' Cedric explains to the stranger. 'He must look after his flock.'

'Mine too,' says the boy in black, smiling at last. 'And very strict. He will be cross if I am late for my lessons.' He sets off walking smartly uphill, away from the church gate, the two lads dashing behind him. 'I do not know what he will make of you two in your strange garb.'

'He will not see us,' says Cedric, simply. His turn to stop the boy in his tracks.

'I assure you, my father misses nothing,' he sighs.

'Sometimes I think he is more all-seeing than God himself.'

'Is your father the vicar, then ?' Adam dares to ask, now that the boy seems more human.

'The Reverend John Patrick Eden, Rector of this parish.' The boy nods, reaching out a hand. ' Robert Gerald Eden, at your service, gentlemen.'

'Pleased to meet you, Robert.' Adam shakes his hand as if it might drop off. Their new acquaintance laughs, 'Gerald,' he says, gently removing his hand from Adam's strong grasp. 'I'm usually known as Gerald.'

'Well, Gerald, I'm Adam, this is Cedric and you're not gonna believe how we can trick your dad.'

# A HAUNTING TALE

Halfway up the slope, all three lads come to a halt as Adam and Cedric let Gerald in to the secrets of the magic mobile. 'We've been into all sorts of places,' says Adam.

'And all sorts of times,' adds Cedric.

'And nobody can ever see you ?' asks Gerald, as the boys slowly climb the slope up to the rectory.

'Only the lucky ones like you,' says Adam, 'the first person to spot us when we move on.' 'Who happens to be twelve years old,' adds Cedric with a smile.

'I am indeed that age,' agrees Gerald, pausing for a moment, 'born in the year of Our Lord 1860.'

'That puts us in 1872, Cedric,' says Adam. Turning to Gerald he explains, ' seventy years back from our last stop.'

'In the middle of World War Two,' adds Cedric, quite the history expert now. 'Sammy took us in to the army camp. Gave me this.' Reaching in to his pocket, he holds out the shrapnel. Gerald smiles as he touches the mangled lump of metal cupped in Cedric's hand.

'Went on for five years, that war,' says Adam. '1939-1945. There'll be a cross in front of the church in a few years time. In memory of the dead of both wars. First World War1914 - 1918. I expect you'll be around when it's put up in 1921.'

'I shall be an old man of 61 by then.' Gerald looks alarmed at the thought. 'Or in the grave.'

The boys stop in front of the huge rectory gates, shut as firmly as the church door.

'Allow me, gentlemen,' says Gerald, opening a little snicket gate on the left. 'Welcome to my home.' Holding the gate in his left hand, he makes a swooping gesture with the right, inviting the boys to step through. Cedric's mouth falls open. Gazing at the elegant building beyond the gates, he can barely breathe, let alone speak. At last, he whispers, 'Do you really live here, Gerald ?'

'I do indeed, Cedric, just as long as my father is rector.' With a kindly smile at his new friend, he goes on, 'One could say it goes with the job, like a farm worker's tied cottage.'

Adam rushes off ahead of them. 'Ceddesfeld Hall, Cedric,' he gabbles excitedly.' Like I told you about. Community Centre. All sorts goes on here in my day, Gerald. In the grounds as well. Fireworks, sport, music, mediaeval fair. Open to the public. Anybody can come in.'

'I'm not sure my father would approve,' whispers Gerald, walking with Cedric towards the beautiful Georgian building. Dark wooden double doors stand closed at the front of the house. Above them, a semi-circle of glass, like a fan, divided into segments. Higher up, a white stone plaque, its Latin words picked out in bold black lettering. At the bottom, some Roman numerals. MDCCXCIII. '1793,' says Gerald, then goes on to explain. 'The rector at the time, George Barrington, had two uncles - very important and very wealthy. They provided this splendid rectory. Uncle Samuel was an admiral, the other the Bishop of Durham, no less – Shute Barrington.'

'I've heard of him !' cries Adam, instantly shushed by the other two. Lowering his voice, he carries on. 'Later on, not sure when, they carved the rectory up and named a couple of bits after him - Shute House and

Barrington Lodge.' Sweeping his arm across from the front door to the left, then left again, he points to the places in question.

'Well, I never !' exclaims Gerald. 'Better not tell mother. She'd never cope without our own private laundry. And Lizzie, our laundrymaid, would be out of work. Shute House, eh ?'

Beckoning the boys to follow him, Gerald heads off, away from the front door of the house, hoping to sneak a look inside the laundry windows.  Just as they reach another fine doorway, out shoots a stream of soapy water, missing their feet by inches.

'Beg pardon, Master Gerald.' A pretty young girl in a mob cap and long grey dress, wipes her hands on a long white apron, as she places her metal bucket on the stone step in front of her.  'Didn't see you there. I hope I haven't wet your good shoes.' Gerald blushes at being caught out near the working area of the rectory, out of bounds to the children of the house.

'Not at all, Lizzie, my dear,' he replies, trying to sound kindly but masterful, like his father. 'My fault entirely, shouldn't have been here.' Picking up her bucket, she bobs a slight curtsey and turns to go back in. 'About time for your lessons, isn't it, master Gerald ?' she asks, with a smile. 'Yes, yes, indeed,' he splutters, aware of the other two lads grinning at either side of him. Unlike Lizzie, who doesn't give them a glance. 'Mustn't keep you, sir,' she says, as she picks up her bucket and steps back in to the laundry. Leaving three lads staring silently at the closed door.

'She didn't see you, gentlemen.' Gerald smiles in disbelief, looking from Adam to Cedric.

'Course not,' replies Adam, totally confident now in their invisibility. 'But I managed to get a pic of you two chatting.' Turning his mobile around, he shows the lads a slightly blurred photo. Lizzie framed in the doorway, bucket in hand, Gerald with his back to the camera. 'Can't really see your face, Gerald,' says Cedric. 'Just as well, mate,' Adam laughs, poking fun at his new pal. 'It was bright red ! You fancy her, don't you, that Lizzie ?'

'I have no idea what you mean,' says Gerald, stiffly. 'She is very pretty, of that there is no doubt.' The other two lads grin at each other as he walks away, leading them towards another part of the house, long and narrow, built of the same golden stone. 'Barrington Lodge,' says Adam, he and Cedric running to catch up with Gerald. 'That's what it's called in my day, anyhow. Is it stables or summat ?'

No longer sulking over the joke about Lizzie, Gerald laughs quietly, worried their conversation might be overheard indoors .
'No indeed ! This is Cook's scullery and kitchen. She's always grousing about the long hike to the dining room. Woe betide anyone who sets foot in there uninvited. Human, never mind horses !'

He takes a peek into the kitchen window, hoping Cook might have some cakes or biscuits cooling on the sill. They're in luck. A young kitchen maid spots Gerald peering through the steamed-up glass. With a quick glance round to make sure Cook is well out of sight, she opens the door a crack. 'What you after, master Gerald ?' she whispers, giggling, as Adam quickly snaps a photo. 'You must have a nose like an elephant. You always know when there's pastries on the go.'

Just beyond the door, on a huge scrubbed wooden table in the middle of the floor, Gerald spots a large black tray. On it, dozens of little open tarts topped with home made raspberry jam, glistening in the heat of the kitchen. Gerald's mouth waters, just at the sight, then he gets a whiff of the sharp sweet fruit. Licking his lips, he leans in closer to the girl, 'Couldn't spare a few of those, could you, Louisa ?'

'Certainly not, master Gerald,' she cries, then drops her voice to a whisper as she tells him, 'Your mama asked for them specially for afternoon tea. Some of the village ladies are calling later and she wants to show off Cook's baking skills.' Listening intently beyond the door, silently willing Gerald on, Adam and Cedric cross their fingers in hope of a delicious, freshly baked jam tart. 'There are mountains there, Louisa,' Gerald persists, 'Mama will not miss two or three.'

All three lads hold their breath. The young kitchenmaid throws a quick glance over her shoulder, then darts across to the table. 'You'll get me shot,' she says, rushing back, her white apron hiding a checked cloth, three warm raspberry tarts inside. 'Make sure you let me have that cloth back before Cook misses it. You know what she's like. Eyes everywhere.'

She gently closes the door and returns to her post in the kitchen. Adam calls out, 'Thanks Louisa !', swiftly echoed by Cedric. 'You're an angel,' adds Gerald, opening up the delicious parcel. All three fall silent again, gratefully tucking in to Cook's delicious pastries. Polish them off in no time. And still feel hungry. It would take more than one jam tart, however tasty, to satisfy the hunger of three great lads, whenever they were born.

'Hey, I tell you what, Gerald,' Adam rubs the last few crumbs off his face and into his mouth. 'This bit here, the old kitchen as was in your day, they say it's haunted.'

'Haunted ?' laughs Gerald, carefully folding the checked kitchen cloth to return to Louisa. 'By whom, might I ask ? The ghost of Cook, searching for her three missing jam tarts through all eternity ?'

Cedric, as usual, puzzled by new words the others take

for granted, waits for help. Adam duly explains. 'See, Cedric, a ghost is somebody who can't rest in their grave, comes back to where they used to live. Haunts the place.'

'Nonsense,' snorts Gerald, 'No such thing. A ruse put about to frighten the ignorant.'

'Hey, thanks very much,' snaps Adam. 'Who're you calling ignorant ? Anyway, what about the Father, the Son and the Holy Ghost ? I bet your father's always going on about them.'

Gerald shakes his head. 'Totally different,' he says. Cedric, a bit out of his depth, to say the least, pipes up. 'So, my friends, are you saying that the rectory kitchen is haunted by a Holy Ghost ?' He looks downcast for a moment, as the other lads burst out laughing.

'No man, Cedric,' Adam explains gently. 'Not a Holy Ghost, just an ordinary one. They can be quite friendly, you know. In my day, they say the one in here, the kitchen as it is now in Gerald's day, sits and chats to you. As long as you're not scared, that is. A young lass in a long dress and a mob cap.'

'Could be Louisa,' says Gerald, suddenly interested.

'Or Lizzie,' adds Cedric, happy to know more about this haunting business. 'Can't imagine either of them dead, though.'

'And then there's the Pickled Parson,' says Adam, warming to his subject now. 'Everybody knows that story. Goes back donkey's years. Have you seen him, Gerald ? Up in the attics ?'

'The servants quarters ?' Gerald replies. 'Of course not. We're not allowed up there, in any case.' Not wanting to spoil the fun, he goes on. 'I have heard the story, though.'

'See Cedric,' says Adam, 'in the old days, well, after your time I should think, but anyway a long time ago ...' Growing impatient with Adam's humming and haahing, Gerald butts in.

'The villagers had to pay a tithe, Cedric,' Gerald carries on with the story. 'The rector got  a tenth of everything they'd grown that year.'

'That does not seem fair,' says Cedric. 'My father would have something to say about giving up any of his sheep. That's why I have to keep a close eye on them. Don't want to lose any, never mind giving them away. Couldn't the rector offer to buy them from him ?'

'I'm afraid it didn't work like that, Cedric,' smiles Gerald, 'even though the rector was very rich indeed and could easily have paid the villagers.'

'Anyway, Cedric,' Adam continues, ' this particular rector ...'

'It may have been John Gamage,' adds Gerald. 'Rector of Sedgefield 1728 to 1747.'

'Aye, whatever,' says Adam, 'well, he hadn't been too well and, it turns out, just before the tithes are due, he snuffs it.'

Seeing both boys looking puzzled, he goes on, enjoying keeping them guessing. 'You know, pops his clogs, kicks the bucket ...'

'I think he's trying to tell us the rector died,' smiles Gerald. 'I rather like those phrases, Adam. Very colourful.'

Just as the boys are becoming engrossed in the story, the laundry door opens. Out waddles a large lady, as broad as she's tall. Wearing a white cap, just like Louisa's, and a long apron over her grey skirt, she carries a bundle of clean table linen, starched and pressed ready for use in the house. 'Good morning,

Cook,' says Gerald, his two companions grinning either side of him, perfectly certain they can't be seen. 'Morning, master Gerald.' Puffing and panting, she clasps the linen close to her ample chest.

'I hope you've no bin pesterin' my girls again.' Gasping for breath, she bustles hastily towards the kitchen door. ' I've told you afore, young man. No use hangin' aroond waitin' on titbits. Anyway, should ye no' be at your studies by now ?' Not waiting for an answer, she clangs the door shut behind her.

'I hope she doesn't spot the missing tarts,' says Cedric quietly. 'Seems a bit of a dragon,' adds Adam. 'A Scottish dragon, at that,' says Gerald with a smile. 'Rules the roost in the kitchen. Mother says she's a treasure. Couldn't do without her.' Adam grins, hanging an arm round Cedric's shoulder. 'The main thing is, mate, she didn't spot you and me. Proves the old magic's still working.'

'I wish I could be invisible occasionally,' says Gerald wistfully. 'Especially at lesson time. I can think of many places I'd rather be than in the schoolroom.'

Adam's eyes light up, as another bright idea creeps in to his head. 'Like the spooky attics ?' he asks. 'You never know, we might see the Pickled Parson

up there.' Fumbling in his pocket, he whips
out the magic mobile. 'This little fella could be the
answer to your prayers.'

'Like Sammy in the army camp !' exclaims Cedric.

'Dead right !' Yelping with joy at the prospect of
drawing another new friend into the web of invisibility,
Adam quickly turns his mind to the all-important
question. 'What number do you think, Ced ?'

Wrinkling his brow in thought, Cedric remembers the
number that did the trick for Sammy. '1-9-4-2-, wasn't
it ? The year we were in at the time.'

'Could that work for me, do you suppose ?' Gerald
asks hopefully. 'Maybe using this year – 1872 ?'

'Or the date on the plaque above the door ? What
was it again ?' Adam rushes across to the front of the
rectory. 'Howay, man, Gerald, you're the Latin expert.
What is it ?'

All three lads line up, their heads tipped back, looking
up at the ornate carving.

'Didn't you say they were Roman, Adam, the
numbers ?' Cedric gazes up at the shapes, totally
mysterious to him. 'We could end up back where we

started.'

'With Marcus Severus, you mean ?' says Adam.

Impressed and doubtful in equal measure, Gerald looks from one to the other of his two new friends. 'Roman times ? You'll be telling me next you've met up with Jesus.'

'Not yet,' says Adam, smiling back at him. 'We'll leave that to you and your dad. For now, I'd be quite happy with the Pickled Parson. What do you say, Gerald, shall we give it a go ?'

With Adam and Cedric on either side of him, each firmly holding a hand, Gerald nods. Taking a deep breath, he carefully calls out the numbers above the door.

'One – Seven – Nine – Three.' Holding the mobile in his one free hand, Adam keys in the four all-important digits. After the final tap, Gerald breathes again. 'What now ? I don't actually feel invisible. Can you still see me ?'

'Of course,' Cedric tells him, expert now in the ways of the magic mobile. 'We are always visible to each other. And to new friends like you that we make on our travels.'

'The question is,' adds Adam, 'can other people see you ?'

'Like my father, you mean ?'

'Tell you what,' says Adam, 'Instead of blathering, why don't we go in through the front door? Chances are, nobody'll spot me and Cedric and if they can still see you ... well, what's the worst that can happen ?'

'I'll be in trouble for being late for lessons.' Gerald smiles. 'I'm used to that.'

# OPEN SESAME

Agreed that it's worth the risk, Gerald slowly turns the large handle and gently pushes open the front door of the rectory. The other two lads follow him in to the impressive entrance hall.

'Oh, bless me, Miss Dulcibella, I think we've a ghost !' The soft Irish accent belongs to a little woman with dark brown curls and a pretty smile.  Her plain black dress with a neat white collar and cuffs reaches to the ground. 'Look'it, the door's come open all on its own, there's clever of it.' A little girl giggles, her blonde ringlets bouncing gently as she helps to close the heavy front door. 'Now, my dear, we'd best get you to your desk afore we're both in hot water, so.'

The kindly young woman and her little charge walk hand in hand towards another dark brown door, softly closing it behind them. The lads stand gawping in silence for a moment, before Gerald whispers, 'Well, at least Miss Jane thinks there's a ghost about.'

'Didn't see you, did she ?' grins Adam. ' Is that your

teacher ?'

'One of them,' explains Gerald. 'We have two governesses, the sisters Bulloch. Miss Jane is sweet and kind, but her older sister Isabella is a holy terror. Came over from Ireland to torment young boys like me.'

'And that's the schoolroom, is it ?' asks Cedric, his voice low. Before Gerald has time to answer, the door flies open again. Clad head to toe in black, apart from a narrow ruffle of white lace at her neck, a tall, bony woman with a sharp nose and pin-prick eyes peers through tiny round spectacles into the vast entrance hall. The boys freeze.

'Not a sign of him, ladies, I fear. We shall begin once again without the bold Master Gerald.' Her high-pitched voice cuts through the silence. 'If this tardiness persists, I shall inform his father, who will, I'm sure, exact some form of punishment.' As she steps firmly back in to the schoolroom, the door slams shut behind her, leaving three dumbstruck boys staring at the door.

'Miss Isabella ?' asks Cedric, very quietly. Gerald nods, pulling a face. 'I'm very glad she didn't see me,' he smiles. 'Now you see why I'm in no hurry to enter the schoolroom.'

'You might like it better in my day, Gerald,' says Adam, smirking. 'Don't tell your father – or that governess woman - but, in my time, that's where people come for a drink. Not water, neither. You know, like a pub, an inn.'

'An alehouse ?' asks Gerald, shocked and amused all at once. 'Miss Isabella would be aghast.'

'A ghost, did you say ?' quips Adam, keen to get back to the main reason for their sneaking in to the rectory in the first place. 'Now we know you can't be seen either, Gerald, how about we nip up to the attics ? See if we can spot the Pickled Parson ?' Turning on the spot, he dashes headlong towards the splendid staircase. Placing one hand on the beautiful curved end of the sloping banister, he stands on the bottom step, looking back at the other two boys.

'Perhaps the back stairs would be a better idea,' suggests Gerald quietly. 'Mother may be upstairs preparing for her guests. I should hate to meet her on the landing, even if I am invisible.' Still eager to make it up to the attics, Adam reluctantly steps back to join the others in front of the schoolroom door. All three boys shudder as the sharp voice of Miss Isabella pierces the silence. 'Now, ladies, repeat after me -

amo, amas, amat,' she intones, her Irish accent sitting oddly with the Latin words, 'amamus, amatis, amant.'

'What's she saying ?' whispers Cedric, grabbing Adam's arm. 'Search me, mate,' he shrugs, looking to the expert for help. 'All about love,' Gerald explains, quietly, 'A subject as foreign to Miss Isabella as Latin to a Hottentot.'

'Surely that little lass won't be learning Latin,' says Adam.

'Just the older girls,' explains Gerald, 'My sister Frances and our cousins Constance and Amy. They're all 13 and 14 years old. Miss Jane will be helping the little one with her sampler. Sewing her alphabet and some improving words on to a piece of cloth. She's only nine, my youngest sister, Dulcibella. It means sweet and lovely, which she is, as a matter of fact. Dulcie for short.'

'We shared a cart once with a Dulcie, didn't we, Adam ?' says Cedric.

'Aye, that's right, Ced, on the Shamrock. Easter Sunday 1922,' Adam replies. 'Don't remember her being very sweet, though.'

'Well, at least we know they're all in there, out of our way, girls and governesses,' says Gerald quietly. 'And father will be in his library,' he whispers, pointing to the door next to the schoolroom, 'preparing his sermon for Sunday.'

'I can just see the Pickled Parson sitting in there, back in the day,' says Adam, quietly, his imagination painting vivid pictures of times long gone. 'The peasants filing past outside, leaving their bits and pieces for him. His missus must have been strong, mind. They say she put his dead body in a barrel of vinegar to stop him going off, you know. Then lifted him out and parked him in a chair near the window.'

'So the villagers would think he was still alive ?' gasps Cedric, astonished at the callous behaviour of the rector's wife. 'And you think I live in the Dark Ages !'

Laughing quietly, the boys follow Gerald along the passageway, creeping past the drawing room. 'Where Mother will be entertaining her visitors later,' says Gerald. 'Minus a few jam tarts,' adds Adam, smiling. Finally, they slink past the dining room, its door as tightly shut as all the rest.

'In my day,' Adam tells them, 'that's the main hall, knocked through into the ... what did you call it ?...

drawing room.'

'Knocked through ?' repeats Gerald, rather shocked.

'Think yourself lucky it wasn't knocked down,' says
Cedric. 'Like lots of other places, I hear.'

'Not the rectory, though, Gerald,' says Adam
reassuringly. 'This is a listed building, just like the church.
Protected, you know ? It's massive, though, isn't it ?
The church couldn't afford the upkeep in the end.
Sold it to the council in 1972.'

'A hundred years from now !' gasps Gerald. 'At least
father won't be alive to see it happen. Or any of us, for
that matter. Walls knocked down ! The schoolroom a
drinking den !'

'And the library, mate,' Adam tells him, feeling a bit
guilty. 'The lounge, that is. Posher. You can sit down to
drink in there.'

'What happened to the rector, then, and his family ?'
asks Cedric. 'And the servants ?'

'They built a new rectory, Ced, along Durham Road,'
Adam explains. 'Modern, easier to keep warm and
that. A good bit smaller than this. And they didn't have
servants by then.'

By now, they are standing in front of yet another closed door. 'Well, thank goodness we do,' says Gerald, reaching out to the door handle. 'They will all be  busy about their duties. We should have the attics to ourselves.' 'Apart from the Pickled Parson,' grins Cedric, as he follows Adam and Gerald up the steep stairs leading to the servants' rooms.

No carpets. Very little light.  Holding on to the walls, the lads feel their way up to the landing. A little low gate stops their way, until Gerald fumbles to find the bolt that opens it. To their left, way above their heads,  a huge round window lets in a few rays of watery sunlight. On the wall in front of them hangs a row of large brass bells, each one attached by a metal coil to a rectangular box beneath.  Within its dark wooden frame and glass front, carefully laid out in two rows, small squares with gold lettering bear the names of many of the rooms they have just sneaked past.

'The bell board,' Gerald explains, 'used to call the servants wherever they are needed. There's another in the kitchen, so mother can summon cook or the scullery maid from the house.'

'Very handy,' smiles Adam, ' I could do with one of them in my bedroom.'

'Cold up here, isn't it ?' says Cedric.

'Only the more senior staff have fireplaces in their rooms,' Gerald tells them. 'Like cook and nurse. And the governesses, of course.'

'So poor Lizzie and Louisa have to suffer ?' says Adam, feeling sorry for the young servant girls from  the laundry and kitchen.

'And the other young ones, I'm afraid.  We have eight servants at the moment, all told,' says Gerald. 'But they all get free board and lodge here and half a day off a week. Not a bad life, really.'

He leads the way. A door on the landing opens to a long narrow corridor. Quite dark. Only the round window behind them offers a gleam of light. As the attic door closes behind them,  they are enveloped in blackness.  'Eyes peeled for the Pickled Parson !' Gerald whispers.

'Could do with a torch,' says Adam. 'Guess what ?' With the click of a button, the mobile phone  provides a blue beam.  Just enough to see a few feet ahead of them. Low down on their right, they spot some metal plates, writing scrawled above them. 'Dining room, kitchen, bathroom,' Adam reads out, bending to make out the words in the beam of his torchlight.

'Chimneys, I think,' explains Gerald, 'so the sweep knows which is which for cleaning.' He reaches out, trying the handle of the first door on their left. No luck. Locked.

'Don't suppose you've got a set of keys on you, Gerald ?' says Adam. 'Never worry,' he goes on, his thumbs already dancing across the keys of the magic mobile. 'It worked at St Ed's, didn't it, Ced ?'

'Open sesame ?' Cedric whispers, hoping that their trusty device will not let them down. Adam points his mobile at the door, taps 'send' and grins. 'Go on, then, Gerald - open sez me !'

The door knob turns easily in Gerald's hand. Three small panes of glass above the door provide a glimmer of light, but the boys are glad of the blue glow from Adam's mobile torch. They step in to a tiny windowless room, the ceiling at one side sloping sharply to the floor. Where there is more height, two narrow beds stand side by side, separated only by an arm's reach. Each has a thin mattress, a couple of grey woollen blankets and one pillow, encased in plain white cotton. In the far corner, a small table with a pottery dish and jug.

'Two of the younger servants  will share this room,' says Gerald. 'Lizzie and Louisa ?' asks Cedric, remembering the sparky young girls he and Adam had met earlier. 'Possibly,' Gerald smiles, feeling like a visitor himself on his first secret venture into the forbidden attics.

'A bit poky, isn't it ?' Adam shoves his hands under his armpits to warm them, shivering in the cold of the tiny shared  room. Hunching his shoulders, he bobs his head down to take a closer look at the lower part of the room. 'Might get some photos here, Ced. Park your bum on that bed. You there, Gerald.' The lads perch on the edges of the narrow beds as Adam clicks away. Two small brown suitcases tucked under the sloping ceiling. A little table with barley twist legs holds a hairbrush and a couple of books with dark blue covers. Woollen shawls draped across a dark wooden chair, one black, one grey.

'Freezing, as well. Do they not have a fire or owt ?' asks Adam. 'As I said, only the more senior staff have fireplaces,' says Gerald. 'And  much bigger rooms of course.' Blowing through his cupped hands to warm them, Adam grumbles, 'I bet  the Pickled Parson doesn't hang about in this this titchy room. He'd freeze to death. If he wasn't dead already, that is.'

'Shall we proceed ?' asks Gerald. 'He could be waiting for us just along the corridor.' Acting tough, but feeling a bit scared in the dark, Adam leads the way out of the tiny room. Last out, Cedric has a quick look back. 'Thank you, girls,' he whispers, quietly closing the door. Adam grabs his arm. 'I wouldn't like to be up here at night, would you, Ced ? It must be pitch black.'

'The servants are supplied with candles or oil lamps,' says Gerald, 'but I agree it must be rather grim. Easy to imagine a ghostly presence floating about.'

The boys cling together, following the eerie blue glow of the mobile torch. Feeling their way along the wall, they soon come to a pair of doors right beside each other. Both with small panes of glass above, just like the first room. 'Take your pick,' says Adam, holding his mobile at the ready. 'That one.' Cedric jabs his finger towards the door on the left. Adam quickly does his stuff with the mobile and, in an instant, they're in.

Facing them, a large round window lets in daylight. 'Thank goodness for that,' says Adam, switching off the blue torch. Maybe brighter, but this room is even smaller than the first, the huge window sliced in two by a plain white wall. The sharp roof line cuts into the space, leaving room for just one narrow bed, placed against the wall,  in line with the corridor outside.

'No danger of getting out the wrong side of that,' whispers Adam, ducking down under a wooden beam.  'Good job they're not very tall, these serving lasses,' says Cedric, standing at the foot of the bed.

Little else to see, apart from  a low table tucked under the eaves, holding the usual jug and dish for a cold water wash. A quick click of the mobile camera before Gerald says, 'Shall we move on, gentlemen ?' The boys don't linger, all three beginning to feel the cold of the attic creeping into their bones. Stepping back in to the gloom of corridor, Adam clicks on the blue light of the mobile.  At once, they spot another door opposite, easily opened thanks to the mobile key. Another windowless room, the dark pierced only by the blue beam of the mobile.

Adam creeps in, ahead of the others, flopping down in a squashy armchair next to a large fireplace. 'A  bit warmer in here when that's lit, I bet, ' he says, making himself comfortable. Above the fireplace, a mantelpiece holds a few simple ornaments, a green pottery vase and a pair of wooden candlesticks. Against the wall, a small but cosy bed, fancy wrought ironwork at the head and foot. To one side, a small brown cupboard  with the customary water jug and dish for washing. Next to it, a small brass oil lamp with a glass chimney.

'A bit posher than the others, eh Cedric ?' says Adam. Prising himself out of the armchair, he clicks a few more photos on the mobile. 'Who lives here then, Gerald,  cook or somebody ?'  'Certainly one of the senior staff,' says Gerald, taking a closer look at the rest of the room. 'Remember, this is my first attic visit, too.'

'No sign of the Pickled Parson yet,' says Cedric, opening the door slightly. Adam joins him, pointing the hazy blue light of the torch along the dark corridor. The three lads stick close together, arriving, in no time at all, at yet another door. A flash of the magic mobile lets them in.  As the door falls open, another huge round window stares at them. Shafts of sunlight stream in.

'Biggest of the lot !' shouts Adam, rushing into the room, clicking away at once with the mobile camera. A matching pair of single beds, each with a framework of shiny brass poles at the head and foot. Soft mattresses and pillows, ample bedding topped by thick counterpanes.

Between the beds, a wooden chest of drawers, the

wrought iron handles a delicate lacy design. On top, a small bible, its gold edged pages bound in black, beside it, a large oil lamp, its brass base topped by a round glass dome. In one corner, a small wardrobe. Alongside, a tall thin mirror tipped back inside a wooden frame, its glass specked with dots of grey.

Near the door, a wooden wash stand with sturdy carved legs. A decorative border of dark green tiles across the back. A large pottery dish, floral patterned, sits in a hole cut out for the purpose. Beneath, a matching water jug.

'This is a bit more like, Gerald,' says Adam, still clicking away. 'Could be for the teachers?' he guesses, spotting a large bookcase under the window. Cedric ventures further in to the L shaped room. Turning to the right of the big round window, he finds a fireplace and mantelpiece.

'Just like in Cook's room,' he says, bagging one of two matching wooden chairs either side of the fire.

'Pity it's not lit,' says Adam, taking the other seat.

Upright but quite comfortable, the chairs are covered in thick dark red material, decorative swirls cut in to make a pattern. Nearby, a round table holds a china teapot with two matching cups and saucers.

'I can picture our teachers in here, taking tea,' says Gerald, 'Though I don't care to imagine Miss Isabella in her night cap and curl papers.' All three lads laugh at the idea of the dragonish governess preparing for bed.

'Shhh !' says Cedric sharply, jumping up from his chair. 'Do you hear that ?' The squeak of a floorboard, the rattle of a door handle, the swish of a long robe.

'It's him,' whispers Adam, 'The Pickled Parson. Told you, didn't I ?' Not sure whether to feel thrilled or terrified, the boys leap from their seats and duck down behind a large travelling trunk. Tucked in to a corner, odd bits of furniture and rugs piled around, it provides the perfect hideaway. Huddled together, barely breathing, they wait in silence for the phantom to appear. The door creaks open. The boys draw their heads in slightly, like three tortoises in a pet shop window.

A dark figure, its head bowed underneath a long hooded cloak, floats into the room. The boys gulp in disbelief, but don't speak a word. Holding aloft a small oil lamp, the vision moves towards the large round window. Reaching out a bony hand, 'There you are, so,' it murmurs, extracting a thick volume from a central shelf of the bookcase. 'Now we may proceed.' Turning swiftly round, the vision disappears through the door, vanishing as quickly as it had arrived. Leaving behind a faint aroma of embrocation.

The boys don't move for a moment, frozen to their spot against the wall. Finally, Adam breaks the silence, in a breathless rush. 'Told you didn't I ? The Pickled Parson ! Never thought I'd see him. Brilliant ! Can't wait to tell the lads at school !'

The tight little group breaks out of its huddle against the chilly wall, Cedric grinning along with Adam in his excitement. Gerald, though, is less convinced. 'I was under the impression that ghosts don't open doors, Adam, they just float through.'

'They can do that, yeah,' says Adam, not wanting to give in to Gerald's common sense.

'I don't want to disappoint you, gentlemen, but that vision was neither pickled nor a parson.' Both Adam and Cedric look crestfallen, as Gerald continues, 'I'm perfectly certain it was Miss Isabella, collecting one of the many dusty old books she uses to bore us to death.'

Not willing to give in quite so easily, Adam insists, 'Well she wasn't wearing a big long cloak when we saw her downstairs, was she ?' Cedric shrugs and shakes his head, not sure what to believe any more.

'She brings it down to the schoolroom every day,' explains Gerald, 'Hangs on a hook like a great black crow. Traditional Galway wool, she says, can't beat it for keeping out the cold, so.' His version of Miss Isabella's Irish accent has them all laughing, the spooky spell broken at last.

'Still pretty scary, though, eh, lads ?' says Adam, raising his arms, his fingers fluttering in feeble pretence of a ghost. 'Not the Pickled Parson, the Gruesome Governess !'

Still laughing quietly, the lads slowly make their way back along the dark corridor. The blue flickering light of Adam's mobile helps them back to the landing and a spark of daylight.  He leads the boys down the servants' narrow staircase. As they reach the door at the bottom, Gerald explains that, before the building of the grand new rectory, an older house stood on the same spot. 'I hoped we might see the Pickled Parson today, but I fear he  departed when the old house burned down. They say he used to wander the secret tunnel between the church and the rectory.'

Adam's eyes light up. 'Can we go there next, then, mate ? Get in ! Lead us to it ! What do you say, Ced?' Cedric, rather less keen on the prospect of more ghost-hunting, sighs with relief when Gerald tells them, 'No longer there, I'm afraid. Filled in by the builders of the new house.'

'Spoilsports !' says Adam. 'Poor old Pickled Parson, nowhere to rattle his bones. Maybe we could nip back a couple of centuries and see if we can find that secret tunnel.'

'A very tempting idea,' smiles Gerald, 'but I'm afraid I cannot come with you. I must look in at the schoolroom before Miss Isabella reports my absence to father.' The boys walk slowly towards the entrance hall, all three glum at the prospect of splitting up. 'Just a minute,' Gerald stops suddenly. 'You could come in with me, as we're all invisible.' The boys are taking in this possibility when the library door opens. Out steps an older, taller version of Gerald, a large book clasped under his arm.

'Ah, there you are, boy !' he growls. 'What's the meaning of this ?' All three boys stand bolt upright and silent as he takes a silver pocket watch from his waistcoat pocket. 'Invisibility must have worn off,' whispers Adam. The rector goes on, 'Once again, Gerald, you are over five minutes late for your lessons.'

'Five minutes ?' Adam glances across at Cedric, perfectly certain their visit to the rectory has lasted much longer. Standing between them, Gerald keeps his head down, glad that the gift of invisibility has not left his two friends.

'I must apologise, father,' he says, his brain racing to come up with an excuse for his lateness. 'I foolishly left my Latin primer upstairs in my room. I was just about to fetch it.' He doesn't move from the spot, rigidly standing to attention, until permission is given. Walking towards the front door, his father casts a final command over his shoulder before stepping out.

'Well, get about your business then, instead of dawdling about here.'

As the door falls shut behind him, the boys relax, their stiff backs softening in relief. 'We'd better be off then, mate,' says Adam, grasping Gerald's hand. 'Don't want to land you in any more bother.' Cedric follows suit, with a broad grin, 'Better not risk the schoolroom.'

'No indeed,' Gerald agrees with a smile, ' I have a feeling Miss Isabella would spot you two even if you are invisible.' He opens the front door a crack, to make sure his father has gone. 'All clear,' he whispers, as his two friends slip quietly out.

'Quick selfie before we go,' says Adam, clicking a final pic of all three of them in front of the broad rectory doors. Still keeping his voice low, Gerald smiles and with a farewell wave, says, 'Goodbye, boys, safe journey. I shall remember this day forever.'

# EACH PEACH, PEAR, PLUM

'Poor old Gerald,' says Adam, as the double doors close behind them. 'I bet he'd rather be out here than in there.' Quietly, they creep along the front of the rectory towards the tall window of the schoolroom. 'Miss Isabella,' whispers Cedric, as they peep through the glass.  The formidable governess stands bolt upright at the front of the room, her three young ladies paying close attention to their lesson. In one corner, little Dulcibella reads quietly from a story book to pretty Miss Jane.

'Here comes Gerald,' says Adam, as the door opens and their friend rushes in, Latin primer in his hand. He hesitates for a moment, spotting the two lads grinning at the window. Adam grabs a quick photo of the classroom and its occupants.

'Sorry Miss Isabella, Miss Jane,' Gerald mutters, taking his seat near the back of the room. With a slight smile and a tip of his head towards the boys, as if to say 'Clear off !', he flicks open his text book. Miss Isabella glares over the top of her glasses. 'Late again, master

Gerald. This really will not do. When the girls are dismissed, you will remain to pay back those missing five minutes.'

With a last nod to their unhappy friend, Adam and Cedric slip away from the window. 'Funny that,' Adam wrinkles his brow. 'Gerald was with us for much more than five minutes. Either Miss Isabella's watch is running slow... or ...' He pauses for a moment to take in the possibility which has just occurred to him '... the magic of the mobile can slow down time.'

'That could indeed be true,' Cedric smiles, no longer surprised by the talented machine. 'Perhaps all our adventures have been no more than the blink of an eye.' 'Cool !' yelps Adam, 'You mean me Sunday dinner might still be waiting for me ?' 'Possibly,' says Cedric, calmly, 'and father may not have missed me from the feld.'

Astonished at the idea of time almost standing still while they flit from one age to another, the boys stare at each other, grinning widely. 'Where now ?' asks Cedric, eager for the next adventure. Pausing only for a moment, Adam decides. 'Thisaway !' He gallops towards a narrow path running alongside the rectory, very close to Gerald's schoolroom. Running headlong through an archway above the path, he yells, 'Race you down the terraces !' As they turn the corner of the building, Adam slides to a halt.

'Woah !' he says, 'This is a bit different. Grassy banks in my day. Great for sledging. No flower beds. And definitely no tennis court. They do themselves proud these rectors.' Cedric follows Adam down into the vast expanse of green where the ground flattens out. Mature trees cast dappled shade. A pond sparkles in the summer sun.

'Told you it was great, didn't I , Ced ?' gasps Adam. Hands resting firmly on their knees, both lads lean forward, out of breath with running. They turn to look back at the rectory, its bay windows overlooking the entire garden, stretching away in to the distance. 'Now, in my day,' Adam explains, 'the garden stops here.' Turning his back to the house, he points across the pond 'And there's a kid's playground over there. Swings, roundabouts, climbing frames, you know.'

Cedric has no idea about these modern playthings, but he does understand ponds. 'Plenty of fish in here, Adam. Feeling hungry ?' Rolling up his sleeves, he crouches down at the water's edge, gently feeling around for a likely meal. Almost at once, his hands

wrap around a plump little fish. 'Gotcha !' shouts
Adam, as Cedric lifts his catch free of the water. Too
slippery though. With an elegant leap, the silvery prize
plops silently back into the water. Not to be outdone,
Cedric tries again. And again. Before finally admitting
defeat. 'Never mind, mate,' says Adam, as Cedric
dries his hands on his tunic, 'anyway, I prefer my fish
battered, with a pile of chips and mushy peas. Tell you
what, how about some fruit ?'

Before Cedric can answer, Adam has shot off across
the garden towards a high wall covered in stout
branches, gnarled with age and spotted with pale
green moss. 'What do you fancy today, sir ?' he asks,
like a market trader at his stall, pointing out his wares.
'We have some lovely apples, pears, plums, even
some choice peaches.'

Reaching out to touch the downy skin of a fruit he's
never even heard of, let alone tasted, Cedric pulls his
hand back sharply. 'Feels odd,' he says, rubbing his
palm against his rough tunic. 'Tastes lovely though,'
Adam laughs, plucking a peach to try. 'Don't usually
grow outside in England, you know. Not warm enough,
even in the summer.' He gently presses the top, near
the stalk, like his seen his Mam do in the supermarket.
'Nah, not ripe yet. Pity. It'll taste like turnip. And give

you gut rot.'

He reaches out to touch the fruit wall. 'Must be heated somehow, Ced. Clever, eh ? I bet nobody else in Sedgefield has one of these. 'Cept mebbe Mr Burdon at Hardwick Park.'  Flattening one hand against the warmth of the red bricks, Cedric uses the other to twist free a small hard apple from a low branch. Its tough skin, with sunray stripes of red and green, gives way to the pinkish fruit inside. 'A bit sour.' Cedric screws up his face before taking another bite.

'Cor ! See what you mean !' says Adam, spitting a mouthful of apple out on to the grass. Further along the heated wall, pears hang low like huge teardrops, their skin the mottled green and brown of autumn leaves. One bite proves their flesh as hard as rock and just as sour as the apples. 'Not ready for eating, Ced, unless you want belly ache.'

Adam looks towards the far end of the fruit wall. 'Howay, let's see if there's a few plums ready along there.' After one mad dash, they stand staring up at an ancient tree, its branches fastened close to the heat of the wall. A rich harvest of plums, some purple skinned, others tinged red and green. 'Gis a leg up, Ced,' says Adam. Stepping forward with one foot to give himself a solid base, Cedric links his strong fingers together, making a cup for his mate to stand on. Up steps Adam, grabbing Cedric's shoulder for support. Reaching up with his free hand, he grabs at the nearest branch, snatching at a couple of plums before leaping back down. 'There you are, Ced,' Adam chucks one plum to his mate and bites in to the other himself. At last, their luck is in. Sweet, juicy, delicious !

'Spot on !' Cedric grins, the pink juice running down his chin. Of course, one plum each is not enough to satisfy growing lads. Flushed with success at finding this treasure trove of fresh fruit, the boys take turns at hopping up to collect more. Very soon they have a huge pile of plums, in all shades of purple, red and green.

'Right, Ced,' says Adam, leaping down for the last time, 'let's call it a day. Better dive in to this lot before the wasps do.' Making themselves comfortable against the warm bricks of the wall, the lads tuck in to their fruit feast. Bathed in sunshine, the garden stretches out ahead of them.

'Much bigger than in my day,' says Adam, spitting a plum stone on to the grass. 'All houses round here now. Thurlow Road, Wykes Close, Eden Drive.'

'Like Gerald !' shouts Cedric. 'And his Dad,' Adam grins. 'All the streets are named after rectors. The Reverend Eden, Canon Wykes, Lord Thurlow. Even the new playground's called The Garden of Eden. Every time I have a go on the swings, I'll think of Gerald !'

Beyond the garden, fields stretch away as far as they can see. Sheep and cows quietly graze. Stooks of corn stand drying in the sun. In the distance, heavy horses pull a simple plough, making rounded furrows of newly turned earth. Whipping out the magic mobile, Adam says, 'Stand over there a bit, Ced, while I get a few shots.' Clutching his shepherd's stick, Cedric looks right at home in the country landscape.

'Now me,' he says, holding out a hand for the mobile camera. Adam grins, passing the phone over. Flinging out his arms, he strikes a dramatic pose in front of the fruit wall. 'Go on then, Ced. Just point and press.' Holding his stick in one hand, Cedric holds the phone aloft with the other. As he presses the square central button, screek ! goes the camera, as Ced takes aim. 'Another for luck !' shouts Adam, reaching up as if to pluck an apple from the wall. As both boys look towards the top of the fruit wall, they see an almost identical pair of lads looking down at them.

'What yer doin' ?' says one. 'Ye'll be in trouble if the rector cops yer,' adds the other. Both lean their grimy elbows over the top of the wall, clinging on like a couple of skinny monkeys. 'How d'you get up there ?' says Adam. 'Easy when ye know how.' One of the lads grins down at him. 'Do it all the time, don't we, Charlie ?' 'Aye,' says his mate, ' you can scrump plenty of fruit from up here. Never been caught yet. Never seen you lads afore, neither.'

'Well,' says Adam, squinting up into the sunshine. 'Lucky for us, most people can't.'

'Unless they are, like us, twelve summers old,' adds Cedric, taking a quick pic of the two lads clinging to the wall.

'Hey, what's your game ?' one shouts down angrily. Hearing the screech of the phone, he almost loses his grip on the high wall.

'Don't worry, lads.' Adam raises a hand to shade his eyes. 'Just one more for the gallery.' Not wanting to scare off the two newcomers, Cedric slips the mobile into his belt pouch. 'Is that where you live?' he asks them. 'Yon side of this wall ?'

'Sometimes,' says one, grinning at his mate. 'Depends

on the time of year, don't it, Robert ?'

'Aye, nice and warm down here in the winter, tucked up against the brickwork. Better than the workhouse any day of the week.'

For an instant, Adam's face is a picture of surprise and disbelief. 'The workhouse ! Like in Oliver ! Here in Sedgefield ? Whereabouts ? What's it like ? Do you have to eat gruel? Were you born there ?  Is it awful ?'

He rattles away with question after question, leaving no room for answers. Cedric smiles patiently, shaking his head at his friend's eagerness to learn. The moment Adam pauses for breath, a deep voice booms across the vast expanse of the garden.

'You boys ! Get down at once ! Be off with you!'  His black frock coat billowing out behind him, the rector comes striding across the lawn.  Dropping like ripe fruit from the top of the wall, the workhouse boys land on the other side. One yells back, 'See you at the farm gate, lads, just past the rectory wall.'

Gathering up the last few plums lying around their feet, Adam and Cedric chase up the grassy terraces, past the impressive tennis court and ornate flower beds. As they rush past him, the rector notices nothing but a sudden gust of air disturbing the peace of the sunny afternoon.

# WORKHOUSE WANDERERS

Running on to the little path at the side of the rectory, the lads dash through the snicket gate and on to the slope leading away from the big house. They hear the two workhouse lads before they spot them. Just as they'd said, in front of the farm gate at the bottom of the hill. Leaning against each other. Laughing, gasping for breath, waving – all at the same time.

'They must be from Ivy House,' says Adam, as he and Ced wave back. 'The old workhouse, where poor people had to live. Used to be down Station Road, till they knocked it down.  New houses there now. With a big tower up the middle, just like in the old days.' Stepping swiftly down the hill, Adam and Cedric soon come close enough to see how poor these lads are. Ragged clothes hang loosely on them. Thin jackets, shiny with age, held together by the odd button. Baggy trousers, cut down short, barely cover their rickety legs.

One wears a soft round cap, his dark hair jutting out in jagged spikes. His bare feet filthy, the nails hard and

black.  'Your turn for the shoes today, in'it Charlie ?' he grins. Adam blushes, aware that he had been staring at the lad's feet in disgust. He and Cedric hand over the remaining plums, sorry they hadn't saved a few more. The workhouse boys polish them off in no time.

'Lovely them,' says one. 'Aye, fest this year,' adds his mate, rubbing his sticky hands on his trousers.

'Take your picture ?' asks Cedric, pulling the mobile from the bag on his belt.

'How about a selfie ?' says Adam, standing beside Charlie. 'Ced, you go to the other end, next to ... Robert, is it ?'

The lad with the hat and no shoes grins. 'Bob,' he says, 'Robert's me Sunday name.' Smiles all round as Cedric clicks a photo of the four of them in front of the farm gate.

He turns the mobile round, showing off his handiwork. Astonished, the two workhouse lads grab each other, pointing at the picture, laughing. 'Never knew I was so good lookin',' says Bob, grinning at his own image. Charlie, staring at the mobile lying in Cedric's hand, asks, 'How did you do that then ?' Pleased at his new-found photographic skill, Cedric smiles shyly, handing the mobile back to Adam. 'Easy when you know how, isn't it ?'

'Yeah,' Adam grins. 'Where I come from, all the kids have them. This one's a bit special, though. Tell you what lads, take us for a look at Ivy House and we'll tell you all about it.' Adam steps away from the farm gate, heading back up the hill. The two workhouse lads look at each other for a moment. 'Ivy 'ouse ?' says Bob at last, 'Never 'eard of it.'

Adam insists. 'The Workhouse, up Station Road, that's where you live isn't it ?' He stretches out an arm pointing up the hill, beyond the rectory.

'No, mate,' says Bob, pointing the other way, 'Workhouse is over yonder, by White Bread Field. Bloody 'ell 'ole. The Spike, they call it. Likely cos it's sharp and painful.'

'Aye,' Charlie adds with a grin, ' and once yer on it yer canna ger off. We can show yer, if you like, but yer won't get us in there again.'

The two workhouse lads set off slowly. Adam and Ced fall into step behind, walking away from the farmhouse, a huddle of poor-looking houses nearby, cow byres in amongst them.

'Better off looking after yersel,' Charlie goes on, defiantly. 'Better than Master 'allimond, any road.' 'Aye and that missus of 'is,' Bob scowls. 'Matron, she calls herself. Dolin' out gruel like watter, only the odd lump to chow on. Standin' in line for a chunk of stale bread and a slop of sour milk. Not me, mate.' They trudge past a row of houses, the rubble stone of their wall showing patchily through the flaking whitewash. Opposite, the smithy, the top half of its stable door standing open.

'Sometimes call in here for a warm,' says Charlie, leaning his arm along the top of the open door. 'Aye, gets a bit nippy come the winter.' Bob looks over his mate's shoulder into the blacksmith's shop. 'Anybody about ?' His shout echoes in the emptiness. No answer. Dying embers glimmer red and orange on the blackened top of the forge. Tools left lying look ready for work, others hang on neat wooden pegs.

'Funny,' Bob shoves black fingernails under his hat for a good scratch of the head. ''e's allus here, smithy, clattering away at 'oss shoes and such like. Sometimes gives us a bite to eat and a sup.' The other lads follow as he lifts the metal door sneck and steps inside the blacksmith's shop.

''es mebbe tekken an 'oss back to t' farm,' says Charlie, picking up some large metal pincers from the forge. 'Back any minute.' Following his lead, the other lads wander further in to the little smithy, having a good look round.  'Pottery in my day,' says Adam, clicking away with the mobile, fascinated by all the paraphernalia inside the tiny stone building.

'We saw the blacksmith here didn't we, Adam?' Cedric  reaches up to stroke the soft brown leather of a horse's harness hanging on the wall. 'Talking to Paddy from the Shamrock.'  'We did aye, Ced,' Adam smiles. 'Easter 1922. Not the same bloke now, though, I doubt. 1872 now, isn't it? Gerald said. Unless we've slipped back a bit since we met you two lads.'

Side by side, Bob and Charlie, slowly turn to look at each other. Without a word, their brows crinkle in disbelief. 'Sorry, lads.' Adam laughs, waggling the mobile in front of their puzzled faces. 'See,' he goes on, 'as well as taking pictures, this little beauty lets us travel in time.'  'And makes us invisible,' adds Cedric, grinning.

The smile soon fades, as tuneless whistling and the thud of heavy boots announce the return of the blacksmith. All four lads stand stock still as he comes stomping into his little workshop. Without a glance at any of them, he heads straight for his forge. A squeeze of the bellows brings back a red hot glow. Using the huge pliers, he picks up a short piece of metal, pushing it deep in to the embers. Sparks fly as he flattens and batters it into shape. The boys watch entranced, the blacksmith totally unaware of his young visitors. After a moment, Bob nods his head sideways towards the open door. All four sneak quietly out.

'Looks like we're invisible an'all !' Charlie whispers. 'Smithy'd have played 'ell if he'd seen us in there when he weren't about,' says Bob.

'Elf and safety?!' Adam grins. 'All the rage in my day. 2015, that is. I've gone back in time, see and Ced's come forward. Anglo Saxon he is, you know.'

Looks of bewilderment return to the workhouse lads' faces. Cedric knows how they feel. 'We've been bouncing about all over Sedgefield's history, haven't we mate ?' says Adam. As they carry on walking towards the dreaded workhouse, he tells their new friends about some of the others they've palled up with on their time travels. Jack from Hardwick Park, Johnny at the ball game, Sammy with his shrapnel,

Gerald, the rector's son.

'Don't forget the lasses, Adam,' Cedric butts in. 'Remember ? Joan and her mates at the almshouses, Edith and the twins moving out to Winterton, Ruby and Dulcie on the Easter Shamrock.' One after another, their smiling faces pop up as Adam flicks through his mobile gallery of photos.

'Did they all go invisible an'all ?' asks Bob, never breaking step.

'Just a couple of them,' says Adam, 'Sammy was chuffed, cos it got us in to the army camp.' 'I've still got his shrapnel, look !' Cedric produces the mangled bit of metal from the pouch on his belt. 'And Gerald took us up in to the rectory attics to see the Pickled Parson.' 'Never turned up though, did he, Ced ?' says Adam. 'You know, lads, the ghost.' 'Believe in them, do yer ?' Bob smiles, tipping a wink to Charlie. 'Ghosts ?'

'Oh, yeah,' Adam gushes, full of enthusiasm. 'I'd love to see one, me. A real one, you know, not just mucking about like at Halloween.'

'Plenty of ghosts round here,' says Charlie. 'If you only have eyes to see them.'

'Right now, all I can see is you two charmers,' Adam grins. 'Come to think of it ...' He stops short, looking back along the road they've walked together. Houses on both sides, but not a soul about. '... we've seen nobody  since we met you lads at the farmhouse gate.'

'Only the blacksmith,' says Cedric casting an eye over the deserted village. Nobody outside the cottages, not a pony and trap to be seen. Not even a stray dog. Adam smiles uneasily.

'Are we anywhere near the workhouse yet, lads ?'

'Not far now, just yon side of East Well House.'  Charlie points ahead. At the end of the street, a whitewashed farmhouse stands alone, fields beyond it on either side. 'But we always swore we wouldn't go back, there, didn't we, Bob ?'

'So me da cud bray us agen ? No fear. Crackpot him. In and out o' prison an'all. An me Ma.   Had to tek the babby in with her the last time.'

'What? Into prison ? A baby ?' Adam is almost speechless with shock. Cedric quietly takes over from him.

'The one up near the church ?' he asks gently. 'They made it a  school later, didn't they, Adam ? Johnny went there. The lad at the ball game.'

'A bit too late for us,' says Charlie, with a wry smile. 'We never had any schoolin'.'

'Started on the wander when we was nine year old,' Bob tells them. 'Just like all the lads. Better than stuck in that place. Open stinkin' drains, rubbish all ower. Sooner be out in the fresh air.'

'You mean, you live out in the open all the time ?' says Adam.

'Rain, 'ail, snow or blow,' Robert smiles. 'Ye sharp get used to it. Better'n bein' out in the workhouse yard all day, brekkin' stones.'

'And nobody looks after you ?' Impressed and horrified all at once, Adam is struggling to think how he would cope with such a life.

Charlie sniggers. 'What, like little bairns, ye mean ? They cannut even get that right. At least our babby never ended up in prison, like Bob's little sister. As soon as our Jenny was born, me Ma had to put her out to a minder in the village.'

'Are you lads not brothers then ?' asks Cedric.

'Why no !' Robert cuffs Charlie gently round the ear. 'If we're both twelve year old, like you say, that'd mek us twins, wouldn't it ? I'm much better lookin' than 'im.'

'Best mates though, blood brothers, eh, Bob ?' Charlie grabs his pal in a friendly head-lock. They tussle for a moment, shoving each other around, play fighting, no blows landing. Adam and Cedric smile at their antics. 'Gone through thick and thin together, haven't we mate ?' Hanging an arm loosely over his pal's shoulder, Bob goes on, 'Shall we tell 'em, Charlie ?'

Folding his arms over his skinny chest, Charlie nods like a wise old man. 'S'pose we'd better.' He stands back silently as his pal begins. 'See lads, we've been coming back here for years. In spirit, like. Even though we hated it when we was alive. '

Adam and Cedric stare open-mouthed, struck dumb as the story unfolds. 'Thing is, we can't show you the old place, cos it's not there no more, thank God.' Bob falls silent as Charlie picks up the tale. 'Always said we'd come back and haunt the place, though. Even after they knocked it down and built a new one.'

'Ivy House !' yells Adam, grabbing Cedric by the arm.

'Like I said, down Station Road. Mind, that's gone, as well, now. In my day, I mean. We don't have workhouses in my day.' 'Or mine,' whispers Cedric, not sure whether to be scared or excited in the presence of his first ghosts. 'Pleased to 'ear it,' says Charlie with a smile.

'Nobody's ever spotted us afore,' Bob smiles broadly. 'Powerful magic in that mobile of yours, Adam.'

'Or maybe,' Cedric offers shyly, 'it's because we're all lads of twelve summers.'

'My gran says you only see ghosts if you believe in them.' Adam's confidence returns now he's used to the idea of ghosts walking about in his company. 'And they're nothing to be scared of. She always says it's the living you want to be worried about, not the dead.'

'Sounds like a wise woman, your gran,' says Bob, leading the little group on towards the farmhouse, standing alone, just as deserted as the rest of the village.

'East Well Farm,' says Adam. 'Still there in my day.'

'That's a mercy,' Cedric smiles as Adam rushes on ahead of the others.

'Butterwick Lane, lads, race you to the cemetery. Plenty of ghosts in there, eh ?' He swings round, a broad grin splitting his face as he looks back at the others. All three still on the spot where Adam left them. Cedric leaning on his thumb stick. Bob and Charlie, each with an arm slung over his pal's shoulder, the other raised in a friendly farewell. Smiling and waving. 'So long, Adam,' the workhouse lads shout in unison, as they begin to fade from his sight. 'Look after him, won't you, Ced ?'

Adam stares in disbelief as the two lads slowly vanish, like pictures fading in an old album. Cedric walks steadily towards his good friend, thumb, as ever, hooked into his walking stick.  'They always said they wouldn't go back, Adam,' he says gently. 'Nothing to go back to.'

The two boys gaze across the empty field where the old workhouse would have stood. Adam sniffs, roughly wiping the back of his hand across his nose. 'Good job they pulled it down. Sounds disgusting.' They walk slowly on, both deep in thought. 'Never thought ghosts'd be like that,' says Adam after a while. 'Just lads like us. Happy enough, an'all, not weeping and wailing and scaring the living daylights out of you.'

Cedric smiles. 'We may meet some more along this road. Plenty at the ... cemetery, was it ?'

'I was joking, man,' Adam grins at last. 'Anyway, we'd have passed it by now. Metal railings all along and a little house at the gateway. Mustn't have built it yet. Pretty full in my day.'

A little further along, he stops, looking across open fields to the left. Pointing into the distance, he says, 'See over there, Ced, that's where my school is. Or will be – in 2011. Sedgefield Community College. Smart as. Kids are fighting to get in.'

'Not like Johnny's school in the old prison ?' Cedric smiles, leaning on his shepherd's crook. 'Not a lot.' Grinning, Adam pulls the magic mobile from his pocket. With a flick of his finger, he scrolls through a series of pictures of the smart new building.

'Pretty cool, eh, Ced ?' Cedric nods thoughtfully as the modern images flash past his ancient young eyes. 'Tell you what,' Adam spins round to face Cedric, 'why don't we go take a proper look ?'

'In your day ?' says Cedric, grinning broadly, 'Cool !'

Cradling the mobile in his hand, Adam lifts a finger to

tap in the next magic number.

'Hang on a minute, Ced. There's a text here. Haven't had one of them for ages.' Laughing, he starts to read it aloud. 'Stuck with history homework. Due in tomorrow. Gis a hand mate.'

He starts tapping in a cheeky reply, chatting away to Cedric at the same time.

'Typical ! He's always doing that. My mate, Jonathan. He's had all the summer to do that project. Leaves it till the last day of the holidays. He's the one I was trying to text when I landed in your father's feld.' Looking up from the mobile, he finds himself alone.

'Ced !' he shouts, looking frantically around. 'Ced ! Howay, mate, stop mucking about !' Quiet at first, his calls grow louder, then softer, as he realises there's nobody there to hear him. 'Not you an'all. Faded away like the workhouse lads ?'

He flips open his mobile. As the gallery flashes past, smiling pictures of all the friends he met on this magic mobile trip, his eyes mist over a little. 'Mebbe you were all ghosts. All them canny lads and lasses.' Roughly rubbing the tears away with the back of his hand, he starts to laugh quietly to himself. Looking up to the skies, waving the mobile aloft, he yells joyfully, 'Tell you what, though Ced, I bet my history project's the best in the whole class !'

Above his head, Adam hears the tinny cry of his mobile phone. The ring tone he chose specially, mainly to annoy his mother. 'Yeah ?' He quickly drags the phone down to his ear. 'Mam ?' As he listens to his mother's voice in silence, Adam's face grows more and more puzzled. 'Half an hour, you say ?' He shakes his head, frowning, but pauses only for a moment before carrying on. 'OK, OK, I get the message,' he snaps, 'I'll be home in two tics.'

Flipping his phone shut, he pops it into his pocket with a wry smile. 'Half an hour, Ced,' he whispers. 'That's all it's been since she last rang, when we were in your father's feld.' The sudden beeping of a car horn makes him jump to safety on the grass verge. 'Watch it !' he yells, as the driver speeds away, flinging an empty drinks can out of the window as he heads off down Butterwick Lane. 'Idiot !' Adam grumbles to himself, stepping back on to the road.

Scratching his head, he slowly looks around. Across to the new school building, its white roof curved like a wave on the ocean. 'Definitely wasn't there before,

Ced,' he mutters, as if his Saxon pal was still by his side. 'Pity you're not around to see it.' The cemetery, houses opposite at St Edmund's Green, more beside East Well Farm, rooftops as far as the eye could see. All the familiar places of his everyday life.

'Must have been that text message that did it, mate,' he says ruefully. 'Sent you back to your time, me to mine.' He wanders homeward along The Lane, remembering the pals from the past he's met in just thirty brief magical minutes. All now whirling around in his memory.

Crossing over Durham Road, he looks across, past the fire station and West Park Lane, to the feld where he first met Cedric. Gently raising a hand in farewell, he whispers, 'What a trip, eh, mate ? Thanks for coming with me. See you around ?' And as he turns to walk away, Adam swears he hears a chorus of sheep bleating, 'Goodbaaahye !'

# GLOSSARY

## A

Ack-ack – anti-aircraft guns fired on enemy planes

Aghast – shocked

Aisle – walkway in church, pronounced Eye - L

Ammo – short for ammunition

Aspidistra – a house plant with very large shiny leaves

Asylum – a hospital for people with mental problems
(a word no longer used)

ATS – Auxiliary Territorial Service – women soldiers in World
War II

## B

Bags I ! – I choose !

Banqueting House – building where special meals were
eaten, another Hardwick folly

Barley twist legs – table legs carved like sticks of barley sugar

Bellows – large air bag, often leather, squeezed to blow air
into the fire

Bigwig – important person, perhaps so called because of
the size of his hairpiece

Black leaded – a way of cleaning old-fashioned cookers

Bray – beat, smack

Brassoed – cleaned using a special liquid polish called Brasso

Breeks – trousers

Bridle – leather straps attached to reins, placed over a horse's head

Brylcreem – used by men to smooth their hair down, popular in the 30s, 40s and 50s

## C

Choir stalls – seats for the official singers in church

Clammin – very hungry (dialect word)

Clippy mat – a small rug hand-made from scraps of old material, especially in the north-east

Crackpot – crazy, mad

## D

Dawdling – standing around, wasting time

Dolly stick – a wooden pole with three 'feet', used for pushing washing about in the poss tub

Doodah  –  nonsense word for something you don't know the proper name of

Draper – shop selling clothes and materials

Dunkirk – a town on the French coast; during World War II, hundreds of British soldiers were rescued from German troops by a flotilla of small boats

## E

Each Peach, Pear, Plum – first line of a skipping rhyme, it goes on 'Out goes Tom Thumb'

Egging on - encouraging

Eaves – long edge of the roof, sticking out beyond the building

Elbow grease – the effort of cleaning something, your elbow going back and forth

Embrocation – cream used to relieve aches and pains, often very smelly

Enamel (labels) – metal covered in a glossy surface, often white

# F

Fizzer – armed forces slang – your name was put on a list if you were in trouble

Flat iron – used like a modern iron, but heated by coals

Flitting – moving house

Forage cap – a small hat worn by soldiers

Frock coat – a long coat, formal, often black, worn by men

# G

Galway – a county in the West of Ireland

Garb – clothing

Georgian – from the time of the early King Georges of Britain 1714- 1830

Get-up – outfit, clothes

Get wrong – get into trouble, told off

Gnarled – twisted and crumpled

Gorgon Medusa – in Greek myth, a monster woman with snakes for hair, killed by Perseus

# H

Hottentot – native from the depths of Africa

Huffed – annoyed, offended

# I

In hot water – in trouble

Itchy dabber – children's game with numbered squares, like hopscotch

# J

Jerry – short for German, commonly used during World War II

Jet – a black gem stone, often found near Whitby

Jif – a moment

# K

Kiln – heated chamber for firing pottery

Knee breeches – smart trousers, half length

# L

Liberty bodice – a sleeveless jacket, buttoned up the front, worn under clothes for warmth

Limpets – conical shells which cling to rocks

Lunatics – people with mental health problems (not used now)

Lych gate – roofed churchyard gate, where coffins would be rested

Lyre – stringed musical instrument, like a small harp, held in the hand

# M

Macaroons – coconut sweets

Matted – pressed into a thick mass, often by mud or blood

Milk churns – big metal containers used before bottles and cartons were invented

Mob cap – a soft circular hat with a floppy brim all round

Motley – mixed, not usually in a good way

Munitions – factories making shells and bullets for warfare (from 'ammunition')

# N

NAAFI – Navy, Army and Air Force Institutes

nada – nothing (a Spanish word)

Nosh – food (slang)

# O

Oojamaflip – nonsense word for something you don't know the proper name of

Ops Room – short for Operations Room, where military planning took place

# P

Paunch – sticky-out belly

Paraphernalia – bits and pieces needed to do a job

Pendant – a piece of jewellery which hangs round your neck

Pinafore – sleeveless tunic worn over a dress

Pit yacker – someone from a mining village, with a very strong accent

Plimsolls – rubber-soled canvas shoes

Pontefract cakes – small, flat circles of licorice, often stamped with their name

Portico – columns along the front of an important building

Poss tub – large metal pot used for washing clothes

Primer – a simple book of basic instruction

# R

Ramrod – used for cleaning a gun barrel, very stiff and straight

Raw recruit – a very young soldier, just starting

Reluctantly – not very keen, unwilling

Rickety – weak, likely to collapse e.g. furniture; also bones, softened by lack of vitamin D

Ringlets – long, rounded curls of hair, often made with heated tongs

RSM – Regimental Sergeant Major

Rolls Royce – a very expensive car, usually owned by the richest people in society

## S

Scrag end of neck – a cheap cut of meat

Scrump – steal, usually fruit from forbidden trees

Sedge –a  grass-like plant with triangular leaves, found in boggy / wet  places

Sergeant major – in charge of a group of soldiers

Side-kick – friend, accomplice, usually less important than the 'main man' (or woman)

Sneck – a door fastener

Snicket gate – a small gate for easy access

Squaddie – soldier

Square bashing – marching in a parade ground

Stand pipe – where people collected water to use in their homes; found in the streets

Swagger stick – a short cane carried by senior soldiers

Sweet cachous – tiny sweets, often flavoured with scents such as violet

## T

Tache – short for moustache

Tardiness – lateness

Top brass – very important people

Treasure trove – precious items found by chance

Trident – a very large fork

TTFN – stands for Tata (goodbye) for now, a catchphrase used in a comedy radio show popular during World War II, ITMA (It's That Man Again !), starring Tommy Handley

# V

Vicar's Dash – path from church to rectory

# W

Whatyacallit/ whatyacallems – used when you don't know (or can't remember) a word

Wolfing – eating fast, greedily

Woodbines – a brand of cigarettes, strong, cheap, popular during World War I and II

Wool gathering – day dreaming

Wrap-around pinny – a large apron, tied at the back, worn to protect clothes during housework

# Y

Yon – beyond ; yon side - the other side

Yonder – in the distance;  over yonder – that way

# Z

Zilch - nothing (USA)

# CONVERSIONS

## MEASUREMENT

A yard is just less than a metre,
so 8 yards = 7 metres; 560 yards = 512 metres

An acre is just less than half a hectare,
so 40 acres = about 17 hectares.

## MONEY

Before decimalisation, there were 20 shillings to £1;

12 pennies to one shilling.

1/6 = 1 shilling and 6 pence

A florin was worth 2 shillings – 10 pence in today's coinage

£40,000 in 1748 would be worth £ 7½ million today

# THANKS

I am grateful to all those people whose memories, knowledge, expertise and friendship inspired and encouraged me to write this book.

Sedgefield seniors Les Butler, Dulcie Claxton and Joan Pyle (nee Davison)

Alison Hodgson, Haydn Neal and other members of Sedgefield Local History Society

Adam Lamb and Jack Turton of Winterton Hospital

members of St Edmund's church and the friends of Hardwick Park

writing friends Joy El-Araj, Fadia Faqir, Avril Joy and Wendy Robertson

and numerous others who have shared stories about their life in Sedgefield.

Special thanks to Walter Howell for his excellent drawings and ideas for the cover

and to Ken Pearce and Carrie Gilroy of Addo Printing for bringing it all together.

Norma Neal
Sedgefield 2015